ÆSTHETICS;

OR,

THE SCIENCE OF BEAUTY.

By JOHN BASCOM,

PROFESSOR IN WILLIAMS COLLEGE

NEW YORK AND CHICAGO:
WOOLWORTH, AINSWORTH, & CO.
1872.

PREFACE.

THE following Lectures were written with a desire to supply the want of an exclusive and compact treatise on the principles of taste.

So many principles have been established in the department of beauty, so much of the mind's action in this direction is understood, as to entitle the subject to distinct consideration; and, at the risk of some offence, we have ventured to style our work Æsthetics; or, The Science of Beauty.

It has been our aim to combine and present in a systematic form those facts and principles which constitute the department of taste, and, as far as may be, to make good its claim to the rank of a distinct science. In so doing, we have striven to render a service to the general reader, and yet more to this branch of instruction.

The present edition is corrected and enlarged as the result of further thought, and new opportunities of observation. The discussion here entered on cannot take the place of a critical and protracted consideration of works of fine art, in each of its departments, but will assist and quicken the mind in this most pleasant, practical labor. Its enjoyment will be much more complete, and its conclusions much more just, when aided by even a partial insight into the aims and resources of art. A discriminating and thus thorough appreciation of the beauties of nature and art is at once an exalted and most agreeable form of mental activity, and will immediately and abundantly repay the attention we devote to it. To aid the ordinary student of the beauties of the external and ideal worlds is our object, and we accept with satisfaction the success thus far of our work.

CONTENTS.

LECTURE I.

LECTURE II.

LECTURE III.

LECTURE IV.

LECTURE V.

LECTURE VI.

LECTURE VII.

LECTURE VIII.

LECTURE IX.

LECTURE X

LECTURE XI.

LECTURE XII.

LECTURE XIII.

LECTURE XIV.

LECTURE XV.

LECTURE XVI.

LECTURES ON TASTE.

LECTURE I.

MOTIVES FOR THE CULTIVATION OF TASTE. — DIVISION OF SUBJECT. — NATURE OF BEAUTY.

THERE is a pleasure connected with every form of human action, and with almost every healthy act, whether it be physical, intellectual, or moral. In the intensity and value of these pleasures there is great variety. On the one hand, there is the glow of a physical system, rapid and perfect in its involuntary functions, which, if not always itself a distinct and definable enjoyment, is yet the condition and measure of many enjoyments; and, on the other, the commanding pleasure of right action, which, in its imperial nature, suffers no comparison or valuation of itself with other pleasures. But not only has pleasure been made the attendant and additional reward of healthy action, though that action have sole reference to utility or duty, not only do the physical and the mental machinery include within them something of the play of music, but a perception has been given us, chief among whose objects is the high and peculiar enjoyment which it imparts, — the perception of beauty.

The fact that this perception is one of the constituents of our nature — a universal and most characteristic element of manhood — would seem to be an adequate reason why we should investigate it, and the principles which control its action, and thus see its relations to character. Without adding to other acquisitions this acquisition also, we cannot fully meet the injunction, Know thyself; nor lay broad the foundations of knowledge in an understanding of that intellect which is at once the recipient and interpreter of all knowledge; nor work into the structure of perfect character that full variety of materials and complement of forces which, in the conception of its Great Architect, were designed to make it the sanctuary at once of strength and beauty. The nature and relations of the perception itself, however, furnish us additional reasons.

A most obvious consideration inviting us to this department is the enjoyment which a cultivated taste is able to impart. As long as the pursuit of pleasure is so leading a trait of man's character, is so prominent among the right incentives to effort, we surely need no other motive or justification of an action than that it repays us by an adequate and innocent pleasure. The gift of a perception, with so obvious and primary a reference to the enjoyment thereby to be conferred, marks the Creator's estimate of happiness, and severely rebukes the indolence which suffers a great faculty to become weak by inaction, and sink from its function and from the circle of powers. The peculiar and abundant pleasures designed to be conferred upon us in this intuition claim our grateful acceptance.

The very nature, however, of the gratification afforded, and its relation to other gratifications, are additional motives for its pursuit. It does not belong to our animal nature, neither to the appetites or passions, but, as a higher and more spiritual enjoyment, can be thrown into the balance against these, and unite its forces with those other perceptions which release us from the sensuous and passionate. The love of the beautiful is often a powerful auxiliary of virtue, by engaging the faculties in an ennobling form of activity, thus at once preoccupying the ground against vicious inclinations, and bringing the mind nearer to the yet higher intuitions and enjoyments of right action. In the contest between the spiritual and physical which is waged in every man's nature, beauty arrays itself on the side of the former, and may often furnish that intellectual enjoyment by which the mind is first brought within the calmer, more profound and abiding pleasures which belong to the strictly rational intuitions. Beauty is often the door-keeper to those charmed precincts within which are truth and right.

A fourth reason why we should render ourselves susceptible to the impulses which arise from a perception of beauty is, that they lend themselves as additional inducements to our best action, in a great variety of directions. The several sciences offer for their pursuit their own appropriate rewards; but not unfrequently do we find a most grateful gratuity in the new beauties which they reveal. Beauty is so inextricably interwoven with truth, that, when seeking the last, we yet inevitably find the first, and with it a new reward and motive of effort. So also is it in the mechanical labors of life. Our work lies amid nature and natural forces, and we cannot with a delicate intuition move in that great gallery of the germs, suggestions, studies, and models of all great work, without finding each step a pleasure. Art may also, in its higher forms, become fine art, and in all its forms call into requisition the rudiments of beautiful expression, in its lines and outlines and surfaces. Thus may pleasure still run through all the wearier passages of life, the love of the beautiful come in as a most welcome impulse, and save our duties from becoming wholly mechanical, an irksome routine, by giving to them the elasticity of a rational sentiment. Beauty, then, is not only with the intellectual as against the physical, but is an ally in all worthy effort, furnishing a new motive to do, and a new satisfaction in that which is well done.

Allied to what has been presented as motives for the cultivation of taste, and yet from its character and importance deserving distinct notice, is the connection of beauty with right, and of discipline of thought in one department with that in the other. The methods of reasoning employed in the discussion of these two classes of questions are similar. This will hereafter appear more plainly. We must for the present rest in the assertion, that, alike in ethics and æsthetics, we are employed with an intuition of the reason, and this, not absolute and unchangeable, but varying with all the new circumstances and relations of each particular case. The reasoning processes by which we trace the immediate influences and remoter results of action, or inquire into its motives and impulses, and thus make ready to pronounce the judgment of right or wrong, are allied to those by which we trace the uses, the interior character, immediate connections, and distant relations of an object, and are thus able to decide upon it, as beautiful or deformed. This similarity in the two intuitions, and in the considerations and reasoning by which the way is prepared for their judgments, unites them closely in their culture.

Beauty also presents a law to action, weaker and more wavering, it is true, than the law of morals, yet one whose observance is a perpetual discipline of the higher nature, — a perpetual imperative resting on the visible life. Beauty, indeed, by an action of the perverted mind and heart, may at this point be brought in conflict with the right, and displace the higher law of duty with its own lower law of taste. A false analysis may resolve right into a certain fitness, and give to ethics no higher obligation than that imposed by the pleasures of good manners and good art. But this very fact, that the one law is sometimes made to displace or obscure the other, only indicates their parallelism, and that beauty, though at a wide remove beneath, yet pursues, in its influence on character, the same direction as the right. It will not often be found that the weaker law is strictly and faithfully applied in all that pertains to daily action, without some respect and obedience directly rendered to the law of duty. The observance of either of these rules of actions will ever constitute a preparation for the observance of the other.

More than this, it is impossible that beauty, in its higher forms and nobler possessions, those of character, should be understood, much less correctly apprehended, without a most thorough knowledge and hearty appreciation of the great law of character, — the right. It is this which gives purpose and form, and thus beauty, to action. It is the vital shaping force of the moral world, and the beauties of that world can no more be understood without its recognition, than those of the vegetable and animal kingdoms without a recognition of the living principles which rule therein. Man must completely drop out of that art which has not schooled itself in his moral nature, since in the right utterance of this lies his beauty. A licentious art cannot be a correct art; no correct art can degrade its object.

Nor would an art without ethics simply lose its prime figure, man, but must be sorely crippled in the poor remainder of its subjects. Architecture in many of its forms has most immediate relation to worship; and surely nature, in her right representation, most directly utters moral and divine attributes, and addresses our religious nature. Art, therefore, not only prepares the way for moral culture; it itself is, and demands, as an indispensable antecedent, that culture.

The amount and kind of intellectual activity called forth commend to us the study and discipline of that part of our nature which finds play in the beautiful. Nor is the lower motive, if we still need it, of the cash value of such knowledge altogether wanting. Good taste, in its restricted and rudimental forms, as a chastened fancy, will find more and more profitable employment in all the mechanical arts, while a frugal elegance in domestic architecture and grounds is to become a very essential element of value. No progress can be achieved without enhancing at every step the price of all tasteful products.

Having seen some of the advantages which attach to a study of the perception and laws of beauty, our next task will be to define some of the terms most frequently employed in this connection, and mark in outline the ground before us. All the definition that we now require, or are yet prepared to give, of beauty, is that it is a certain quality of things and acts. Taste is that power of mind by which we perceive this quality. Taste has come to be intimately associated with criticism, and the last is often regarded as only the application of the first to the various products of art. Beauty, though a leading, is not the exclusive, object even of the fine arts; there may, therefore, be qualities in many productions besides that of beauty which come under the discussion of criticism.

Criticism, then, though finding a most important criterion of excellence in the decisions of taste, is, in the rules and principles of its judgments, possessed of a much wider range than that of any single department. It is the application to products of the tests of excellence in any or all directions.

Æsthetics and the science of beauty may be regarded as interchangeable expressions. All that pertains to the faculty taste, on the one hand, and the object beauty, on the other, to the action of the one or the principles determining the presence of the other; all that constitutes knowledge, science in this department, may be regarded as included in the term æsthetics.

In this use, the word has passed beyond its etymology, and no longer has reference to sensation, nor even exclusive reference to the quality of beauty in sensible objects, but equally includes that quality whether the attendant of sensations or intellections. The original force of the word only serves to mark the great avenue through which beauty has entered the mind, — the field which it has most habitually and widely occupied. All our later progress must serve to define æsthetics by showing the extent and kind of knowledge which belong to it as a science.

We first need to determine, and, as far as may be, to define, the quality beauty, that we may apprehend the object to which every discussion will pertain. Since beauty has no absolute existence, but only exists as the quality or attribute of objects, we shall inquire to what objects it belongs, and what it is in those objects which gives it expression. As the complement of this inquiry, we shall wish to know the organ, the faculty, through which this quality is received by us. Later we shall discuss the principles which determine its presence or absence, and, as a practical application of the truths so established, we shall treat briefly of those arts, termed fine arts, in which the principles of æsthetics find fullest employment.

Beauty is the sole object of æsthetics. No other quality, save as it is either productive of this or tends to destroy it, will occupy our attention. Beauty stands to æsthetics in the same relation as the notion of right to ethics: it constitutes the department; and, however great the variety of modifying circumstances, influences, and relations to be considered, these all are considered in their bearings on beauty; the decision of every question is at this point.

The ingenuity, utility, and novelty of objects may enhance the interest we feel in them, or the value we put upon them; but these and kindred qualities need ever to be distinguished from beauty, however intimately beauty may, in particular cases, be associated with them.

In defining beauty, we say of it, first, that it is a simple and primary quality. It is uncompounded. No two or three qualities in any method present can by their combined effects compass it. No analysis can resolve it into other perceptions, but there always remains something unresolved and unexplained, which is beauty. This is proved by the fact, that the most successful of these resolutions, while they hit on qualities frequently concomitant with beauty, and intimately related to it, are never able to go beyond this companionship, and show the identity of those qualities with beauty, whenever and wherever found. Unity and variety are qualities usually, I think always, in some degree present in beautiful objects. But though this presence may show them to be a condition for the existence of beauty, it does not show them to be its synonyme or equivalent. In fact, we find that these qualities exist in very many things which have no beauty. Their range may include the field under discussion, but it certainly includes much more, and thereby shows that these qualities do not produce the distinguishing and peculiar effects of æsthetics. Thus is it with every combination of qualities into which we seek to analyze beauty. Either phenomena which should be included are left unexplained, or phenomena which do not belong to the department are taken in by the theory. These analyses, either by doing too much or too little, indicate that the precise thing to be done has not been done by them, and only prove a more or less general companionship, and not an identity of qualities. It is one thing to show that certain things, even, always accompany beauty, and quite another to show that these always and everywhere manifest themselves as beauty, reaching it in its manifold forms, and leaving nowhere any residuum of phenomena to be explained by a new quality. The idea of beauty has been with patient effort and elaborate argument referred to association, thus not only making it a derived notion, but one reached through a great variety of pleasurable impressions. It is plain, however, that association has no power to alter original feelings, but only to revive them. If beauty is not, therefore, as an original notion or apprehension, intrusted to association, it cannot be given by it, since this law of the mind has no creating or transforming, but simply a uniting power. Association can explain the presence of ideas, not their nature.

On this theory, beauty must chiefly be confined to the old and the familiar, since upon these association has acted, and be correspondingly excluded from the new, as not yet enriched by its relations. This is not the fact. The beauty of an object has no dependence upon familiarity, but is governed by considerations distinctly discernible at the first examination.

In individual experience, it is a matter of accident what objects shall become associated with pleasant, and what with unpleasant, memories; and in community, association is as capricious as fashion. No such caprice, however, attaches to the decisions of taste. A uniformity indicative of many well-established principles belongs to these. So far as beautiful objects have been united by a firm association with wealth and elegance, this association itself must be explained by their prior and independent beauty; beauty has occasioned this permanent preference, and not a groundless preference this beauty. The simplicity of this quality is seen in the presence of an unexplained and peculiar effect, after we have removed all the effects which can be ascribed to the known qualities present.

It is underived. The primary nature of beauty presents a question of some difficulty, since there are qualities with which it is often so intimately associated that its own existence in particular cases is dependent on theirs, and within this limited range it has the appearance of a secondary and subsidiary quality. In many things, their relations to use give limit and law to their beauty, and, as we here find the impression of beauty dependent on an obvious utility, coming and going therewith, it would seem an easy and correct explanation to refer this peculiar intuition and feeling to the perception and pleasure of an evident adaptation of means to an end in the object before us. The error of such a reference is clearly seen, however, in another class of cases, in which this quality is found to have no such connection with the useful, and to exist in a high degree with no reference, or with a very obscure and remote reference, in the object to any use. If we undertake to deduce beauty from any quality or relations of things, however successful we may think ourselves in a few chosen instances, we shall find a large number of objects which our theory should explain, beyond its power. A more careful examination of the very cases on which we rely will show us, that, while beauty may exist with, it exists in addition to, the quality from which we would derive it; that the utility with which it is associated is not a cause, but a temporary condition, of its existence, or rather that the same relations of the object include and determine both its beauty and its utility.

As it follows, therefore, in regular sequence, no one quality or set of qualities, we say that it itself is a primary and simple quality. There is involved in this assertion an inability to give any explanation of the attribute, or any definition of the word by which it is expressed. It is compound and derived things which can be explained. Simples can only be directly known and felt. Any explanation involves a decomposition of the thing explained, a consideration of its parts, and thus an apprehension of it as a whole; or the reference of it to some source or cause whence it proceeded, and in connection with which it is understood. But no simple thing can be decompounded and explained through its parts; or primary thing be referred as a derivative to something back of it, and thus be explained in its cause.

Nor is the word by which such simple is expressed capable of any other definition than that of a synonyme. A definition must include one or more characteristic and distinguishing qualities by which the thing in hand is separated from all others.

But in the case of a simple there is but one quality, and that alone can be mentioned, and this is to name a synonyme.

All knowledge, therefore, of that which is simple and primary, whether in perception or intuition, must be direct. Mind must interpret mind, and only by the interpretation of similar faculties can this class of properties be apprehended. Certain original perceptions and intuitions must be granted us as the basis of every defining and explanatory process, and explanation cannot go back of its own postulates to throw light upon starting-points. Senses and faculties directly conversant with qualities the same for all, are these postulates. All simple and primary notions and attributes are directly known through these faculties, and the language which expresses them is only explicable to those who have the key, the chart, of kindred faculties. The term beauty is susceptible, then, of no definition, and the quality beauty of no further knowledge and explanation than that which the very power by which we perceive, feel, know it, is able to give.

The conditions and relations of such an attribute may still invite our attention. Nor does the simple and primary character of beauty exclude our second assertion, which is, that this quality is reasonable; that is, a quality for whose existence a reason can be rendered. Certain other qualities occasion it to exist, and these may be pointed out. Right is a primary quality, yet all our judgments of right proceed on certain premises which sustain them, and which can be rendered as a reason why we suppose this characteristic of action present. Thus beauty, when present, is so through causes which can be more or less distinctly assigned, and is not, like the properties of matter, merely known to be, without any knowledge of that which occasions them to be. The proof of this is in the fact that there are questions of beauty, by the concession of all, admitting and calling forth discussion; that men not only discuss points of taste, but are persuaded by the reasonings employed. Indeed, if it were as true of intellectual as of physical tastes, that there is no disputing concerning them, our whole department would be at once annihilated, and fall back among the things incapable of explanation and knowledge. Our progress, and the propriety of every effort toward progress, rest on the assertion, that beauty is a subject of reasoning, and is, in its existence, reasonable. The important and pregnant nature of this assertion will more and more appear as we advance, and its truth will be involved in the very fact, that, following in the steps of all who have preceded us, we make evident that we regard beauty as a reasonable quality, by actually reasoning concerning its existence and the manner of its action.

LECTURE II.

EXPRESSION THE SOURCE OF BEAUTY. — KIND OF EXPRESSION.

THOUGH the simple and primary nature of beauty excludes all analysis and derivation, it does not shut us off from an inquiry for those things which mark, limit, or are in any way the conditions of its existence. In pursuing our effort, therefore, to apprehend and restrict as far as possible this quality, we find, as the first condition of its presence, expression, — the utterance in visible or conceivable form of some thought and feeling. In such forms alone is the incarnation of beauty, and without them it has no individual and localized existence. The thought and feeling which have entered into the composition of any object, and which there find expression, are not its beauty, for they still preserve their own nature and characteristics, and may be known and felt without the entrance to the mind of that higher intuition and emotion occasioned by beauty; nay, more, they may, in many objects, exist dissevered from this quality. These thoughts and feelings are rather the basis, the substance, of which beauty is a new attribute. The strength of an oak may be discerned, and its long and successful struggle with the winds, without the impression of beauty arising, though these are the very things which once seen in the oak secure or enhance that impression. An apprehension of subsidiary qualities, even in their more expressive forms, often exists with little intuition of the beauty which belongs to them, and when this attribute is seen, it implies the action of a new faculty taking cognizance of a new quality. A peach may be known so far as it effects all the other senses, and yet not be known to the sense of smell; and when we discover that the impression of fragrance is only made by those peaches that are ripe, we do not thence infer that ripeness and fragrance are the same thing, but that fragrance is a newly discovered quality of a ripe peach. So, in the action of the reason, is beauty a newly discovered quality of an object expressive of thought and feeling.

Expression, without being beauty, is that in objects which alone gives them beauty; and those things and conceptions alone are beautiful which are expressive. Right is an attribute of intelligent and free action, and of nothing else. There must be an action, and intelligence and freedom must belong to that action, before there can be discerned in it this new intuition, right. An act is one thing, freedom, intelligence, and right are three distinct qualities; but two of these must be present in any act before that is found in which the third can inhere. Right, then, demands, as the basis of its existence, as that to which it can alone belong, action free and intelligent, though freedom and intelligence are conceptions wholly distinct from the right. Truth belongs to a proposition. This we may figuratively say is the substance of which truth is a quality. Not that every proposition possesses it, but that propositions alone can possess it. There must be an assertion before there can be a truth. The assertion is separable from the truth of the assertion, though the first is the condition, the substance of the last. Thus is it with the expression in objects which are beautiful. An object, ideal or real, must be, and thought and feeling must belong to that object, before we have the basis to which beauty may belong. These, however, may exist without beauty, and when beauty exists with these, it exists as something in addition to them. That there must be some object, either in imagination or fact, either in substance or in action, to which beauty may belong before we can possess this quality, none will deny, since there is no abstract, but only a concrete existence possible to the beautiful. Nor is it difficult to prove that there must also be present in this object some thought and feeling. If there is no thought contained in it, the object is meaningless, without designed relations within itself, or with the objects about it. It can, hence, excite no definite feeling, since it has given no direction to the intellect, and can only be an object of total indifference. If beauty could attach to such an object, it would, as an emotion, be wholly irrational, since utterly unable to give for itself any reason, or assign to itself any law or mode of existence. By the supposition, the object called beautiful is vacant of all thought, and hence of all significant relations, and can in itself furnish no ground for any reasonable emotion. We might call an object, within the sense of taste, sweet or sour, or pronounce it to the sense of smell, fragrant or offensive, since these are sensations which demand no other explanation than the mere naked presence of an object. We have no such insight into the properties of matter, as either to anticipate what will be its effect on these organs of sensation, or to render a reason for that effect after it has occurred. Sensations are not reasonable in the sense that any reason can be given why the object present should so affect the sense. Any object, therefore, how little soever the knowledge may be which we may possess of it, may occasion these, since sensations exist without any assignable reason for them save the mere presence of an object.

We are not asked why an apple is sour, nor do we render any reason to ourselves for its making this impression upon us. We are asked, on the other hand, why we regard an object as beautiful, and often seek for our own satisfaction the precise qualities and relations which occasion this impression. Beauty, unlike a sensation, is a reasonable emotion. We confirm or abandon our opinion through reasons rendered, and ever feel that there is something in the object we think beautiful which occasions our judgment, and would justify it to others, if by a successful analysis we could rightly reach and present it. We always feel, and are often able to express, that in an object which makes it beautiful. That which has in it no expression cannot give rise to a reasonable emotion because it can furnish no justification or explanation of it, and we should be compelled to abandon the emotion the instant its validity should be questioned.

That expression in objects, the thought and feeling contained in them, is the basis of beauty, is also shown by the fact, that precisely as any object is rich in appropriate expression does it become beautiful. Inorganic matter has in it comparatively little thought, little work which is the obvious realization of thought, and hence it is relatively feeble in beauty. It may exist in grand dimensions, and express power; in regular arrangements, and express the truths of mathematical figure; in brilliant and transparent gems, and ally itself to light in its pure, quickening character, and thus obtain that utterance which makes it beautiful. But it is only as an aggregating, arranging, cleansing work is seen to have been done in it, by which it ceases to be simply inert, passionless, unshaped matter, that it gains expression, and with it beauty. A brilliant sunset is indeed wonderful in the multiplicity and variety of its suggestions, but only in proportion as the mind is open to these, and affluent in its receptive powers, will it apprehend or feel the true character of the scene.

Organic matter, both vegetable and animal, presents a new and most subtle power. Form now becomes everywhere definite and peculiar. A complexity of parts and members is yet reconciled in an obvious simplicity by the unity of the individual. All relations, both of members within the organism and of the organism to that which is without it, become determinate, fixed, and important. Plan is more rigid, design is more apparent, labor more severe and complete, and, paradoxical as it may seem, liberty and variety more obvious, in the ease and felicity of every new adaptation within the stern limits which the principle of life everywhere assigns itself. This all is but the presence of more expression, the embodiment in the plant and animal of more thought, more purpose and interest. We find the variety, universality, and depth of beauty proportionately increased, and that, as the department of life has been made richer in all that expresses the immediate presence of mind, so is it correspondingly richer in objects of taste.

It is scarcely necessary to trace further this connection of expression and beauty in rational life, so obvious is it. In man we have not only the thought which God has wrought into his marvellous constitution, but he himself is a second centre and source of thought. Through that complex, varied, and most expressive organ, the countenance, and through action, thought and feeling are finding a constant manifestation. If these are a condition of beauty, we should expect to find those features which are the seat of a rational spirit, and that character which is its most immediate product, the high places of beauty. Nor are we disappointed. Of all sensible objects, the human countenance has received the most profound admiration, and of ideal objects, character, as uttered in feature and act, has been the latest and severest study.

That expression in objects is the occasion of beauty is further shown in the forms which art presents and assumes. The painting is primarily judged by the thought which it proffers, by the nature and character of the emotion it contains. Says Ruskin: "Greatness of style consists in the habitual choice of subjects of thought which involve wide interests and profound passions. Style is greater or less in exact proportion to the nobleness of the interests and passions involved in the subject. A natural disposition to dwell on the highest thoughts of which humanity is capable constitutes a painter of the highest order." No painting can be beautiful without expression; — and no criticism is so sweeping and destructive as to say, of any product of art, it is meaningless, destitute of language. Architecture struggles by magnitude to introduce a sense of power, and, by its broken and changing outline, a sense of fulness and variety of resources. A search after feeling and thought as lurking in all that is beautiful is everywhere apparent in poetry. Simple description never satisfies an impassioned nature. It penetrates appearances, reaches for the expression in its objects, and lights its own emotion by the emotion therein contained. Of this all fine poetry is a perpetual example.

"With cowslips wan, that hang the pensive head,
And every flower that sad embroidery wears."

"Mountains on whose barren breast,
The laboring clouds do often rest."

"Thus sang the uncouth swain to th' oaks and rills,
While the still morn went out with sandals gray."

"I hate the dreadful hollow behind the little wood,
Its lips in the field above are dabbled with blood-red heath,
The red-ribbed ledges drip with a silent horror of blood,
And echo there, whatever is asked her, answers 'Death.'"

"I come from haunts of coot and hern,
I make a sudden sally,
And sparkle out among the fern,
To bicker down a valley."

"We parted: sweetly gleamed the stars,
And sweet the vapor-braided blue,
Low breezes fanned the belfry bars,
As homeward by the church I drew.
The very graves appeared to smile,
So fresh they rose in shadowed swells;
'Dark porch,' I said, and 'silent aisle,'
There comes a sound of marriage bells."

If, then, art is judged by the emotion which it raises, and if its aim is to comprehend and bring out the emotive power of all that it presents, it is evident that art at least perpetually recognizes the truth, that expression is the condition of the existence of beauty. We have hitherto said, that thought and feeling are the basis of beauty. It is evident that this is not true of all thought and feeling. We wish now, therefore, to restrict the proposition still further, and show more definitely the kind of expression required.

The inquiry upon which we now enter is one of more difficulty. So many and varied are the emotions which directly, or by more remote association, are contained in beautiful objects, that it is not easy to divide them into classes, or affirm of them any common characteristics. As feeling does not arise except on an occasion furnished in some appropriate object, and as this object involves an intellectual apprehension, we have coupled the words thought and feeling as the two elements of expression. It is only, however, those thoughts which awaken definite emotions, which do not tarry in the intellect, but call forth the feelings that claim our attention. A mere truth as such is not the basis of beauty, but only that truth which is the occasion and companion of feeling. If we know the kind of feeling which must be found in objects termed beautiful, we therein know the thought, since thought is sufficiently defined by the feeling to which it gives rise.

As beauty itself occasions a pleasant emotion, it might seem safe to say, that those feelings which give rise to it must also be pleasurable. This, however, is not a correct inference, since emotions unpleasant to their subject are not always displeasing to the beholder. Sympathy with suffering, sadness in view of a deranged moral system, remorse under a sense of personal guilt, are all unpleasant emotions as felt, though often grateful as witnessed. We are not, therefore, at liberty to draw so general a conclusion as this, that only pleasant feeling will be the basis of beauty; much less the conclusion, that all pleasant feeling will give rise to this quality.

So far as any vicious indulgence is a source of pleasure, it is an object of hearty reprobation, and in whatever object presented will fail to gratify a correct taste. In this direction is it, however, that we may find a general clew to guide us.

In the inorganic world, we reach expression only as there is an approach to order and form, only as the creative power is seen to go further than naked existence, to shape into something that which has been made, to bring out of mere material a workmanship with its interior and exterior relations, with its qualities and uses. Those things which mark the presence of a power which aims not only to do, but to perfect that which it does, to unite it by mutual ministrations into a whole, and to carry it on in a growth of powers to a nobler service and more inclusive end, give expression and beauty to a world which were otherwise a heap of fragments, a chaos of uncompounded elements. All, then, in the inorganic world which speaks the presence of a creative and arranging thought is fitted to give pleasurable emotion.

Sometimes this comes out in a mode of action, in an obscure relation of forces, in that which is only discernible and apprehensible through the protracted action of the intellect. It, when reached, presents itself as a truth, and gives us the pleasure of a new truth. Ocean currents are of this character. The eye never takes them in, the imagination feebly constructs them, the mind alone conceives them, and, as the result of its research, receives the impression of contrivance and wisdom. At other times, the progress in the formative thought is open to the sense, as it were, is seen immediately present in an object controlling and shaping it.

Such an object presents itself as beautiful, and, while engaging the intellect, acts most directly and strongly on the emotions. The veining of marble lies in the sense simply, needs no effort of comprehension, and leaves the mind open to receive its expression.

Anything in the inorganic world which indicates regression and opposition is in itself not pleasant and not beautiful. From the dust of all decomposition the thought escapes, and with it the beauty. The chains which bind these are order and composition. That, then, in the inorganic world which pleases, and, when obviously presented, gives rise to beauty, is progress in plan, something more given to the mind, a fresh realization, by which the chaotic becomes the created, and the created the perfected. All reverse movement, though for the time being expressive, as quickly destructive of expression, is painful. The limitation which this statement requires will appear hereafter.

It is evident, that, with growth in knowledge, the thought contained in things will become more apparent, less the object of investigation, and more of intuition, and that, concurrent with this change, much beauty before concealed will become patent to the observer. The previous discipline of the person must often determine whether many things, both in art and in nature, will be regarded as beautiful. Thought which is partially concealed, through a want of an intimate knowledge of its appropriate signs, may laboriously occupy the intellect without much quickening feeling, while familiarity with truth and that which expresses it may make a scene or an object, mute to most, a lively revelation. Much beauty, both in art and nature, is laid open by a direct perception of qualities first reached through protracted study.

When we pass into the region of life, the relations of things become more definite, and the principle we have partially traced becomes clearer in its manifestations. The plant and the animal have in them a new force far in advance of all that have preceded it, much more distinct and determinate in the form to which it gives rise, involving much subordinate action, various parts and functions within itself, various dependencies and duties without itself.

The plant and the animal, containing within circumscribed limits a most complex and successful plan, with nothing superfluous or deficient, are much more purely, immediately, and sensibly the product of thought than matter. The progress of creative, formative power is here strongly marked, and with this increase of expression, the inquiry recurs, What kind of expression is the basis of beauty? and the answer to be given is essentially that already given in inorganic matter.

That which marks the action of a vigorous, vitalizing power, which indicates the easy and perfect control of the living force over all the matter within its reach, transforming, purifying, coloring, and arranging it by its own subtile efficiency, awakens the feeling of beauty. Many of the processes of life, its various organs, the relations of these, and the function of each, are matters for the intellect, requiring careful investigation, and are presented to the mind, not as immediately seen in the object, but as learned to be in it through the mind's action. The internal organs of the animal are a subject for protracted study, and the mind may take great satisfaction in the truths reached; but there is usually in them no opportunity for such direct perception of fitness in form and completeness of office as to excite the idea of beauty. Those plants and animals are deemed beautiful, the symmetry of whose compacted parts, the felicity of whose distinct members, and whose adaptation to their method of life and local surroundings, are clearly discerned. Increased knowledge is always found to enlarge the number of objects regarded as beautiful, because it enlarges the qualities and relations which perception gives to the mind. Anything which the mind comes to see as obviously indicating the presence and perfect control of the vital power, as the place, color, form, or action assigned a member, it will, unless overruled by some unfavorable association, regard as beautiful. Some animals, as the horse and lion, present themselves at once with a life so compact, forceful, and symmetrical in its members, so evidently within the animal's own wielding, as to be instantly pronounced of all beautiful. The fish, on the other hand, needs to be interpreted by the element in which it moves; and, at play in the water, by its agility and adroitness, by the evident mastery of the vital force over these new conditions, it, too, becomes beautiful.

If any plant or animal is regarded as ugly, it is, —

(*a.*) Because in the individual or species there is deficiency, some falling short of the generic type, by which weakness of the vital principle, a partial triumph of inorganic tendencies is indicated; or,

(*b.*) Because the plant or animal is not seen in its true element or position, and thus is not truly seen, — seen in the adaptation and relation of its parts; or,

(*c.*) Because some association overrules the mind in its judgment.

We shall speak of each of the three occasions of ugliness, and shall find them to proceed on the principle already presented, that beauty is present in all the obviously successful products of a creative, formative power.

In the first case of ugliness, the words by which we must frequently characterize it — awkward, overgrown, one-sided, deficient, deformed — all indicate some embarrassed action of the living force; that it has not completely vitalized and controlled the material which it has taken within its action; and that this inability to execute its plan, this stammering and falling short in the utterance of its message, give pain. The fact also, that any disease or decay in the plant is so much more offensive than any deficiency in the inorganic world, and that deformity and decomposition in the animal are still more offensive than in the plant, show with what increase of feeling we value and cherish these higher products of creative power, and with what sensible emotion we see them slipping back from the vantage-ground once gained by them. The victories of life we joy in; the victories of death we mourn over.

Of the second form of ugliness, — that belonging to a plant or animal out of its place, — sea-plants and water birds often furnish an illustration.

The vegetation, seemingly half inorganic, which hangs like matted hair on the brow of some rock from which the tidal wave has for a moment withdrawn, would, in its dull colors, flatulent stems, and unusual forms, hardly be thought to possess any excellence; but when the ocean has returned to these plants, and, opening their ranks and spreading their foliage, they stand in the deep sea-green, a mimic, flexible forest, pulsing, not to the winds, but the waters, few can fail to call them beautiful.

The heron among land or air fowls seems to be lengthened out of all proportion and adaptations, and to be utterly destitute of every grace; but when seen in the marsh stalking amid its tall reeds or wading the sluggish stream, shooting its reed-like neck and strong bill as a flint-headed arrow after its prey, the effect is very different. The sense of beauty is present when the design is seen.

The third form of ugliness, which will be found to include cases not already explained, arises from association. Of this we give, as an example, the pelican. The pouch of this animal will be felt to make it a homely bird. Though the intellect may fully understand the office of this appendage, and its adaptation thereto, it still allies itself in the senses to that which is inorganic or diseased. It seems an empty sack without vitality, or an unhealthy tumor, and the intellect cannot overrule so strong and universal an association. In some animals, their dishonorable office and localities prejudice us, and in others, their real or supposed noxious qualities. Our ignorance, our superstitions and early impressions, will evidently be fruitful sources of these destructive associations.

From what has been presented, we think we are entitled to advance as a general, if not as an absolute truth, the assertion, that the kind of expression in the organic kingdom, which is the basis of beauty, is that of a perfecting vital power. In proportion as this vital force is complete, controlling the material, form, color, and arrangement of its products, putting its seal upon every particle, is the product beautiful. The easy, ample, accurate way in which the organic end is reached, the mastery of resources and delicacy of finish, which mark a power in love with its labor, are here the insignia of that perfection we term beauty. We have still further to speak of the moral world, and the reflex influence which this must exert on that below it. It is sufficient for the present to have shown that beauty is found with order in the inorganic, and with life in the organic world.

LECTURE III.

BEAUTY IN MAN.—THE EFFECT OF SIN.—REFLEX INFLUENCE OF MIND ON PHYSICAL BEAUTY.

WE have one more important step to take in answering the question, What kind of expression is the occasion of beauty? to point that out in rational action, in character, which gives rise to this emotion. We have seen beauty on the side of truth and life, we shall now see it on the side of right. In order to understand what is uttered by God in man, and what is uttered by man in his own actions, we need to know man in his spiritual and intellectual nature. As an organic being, as an animal, he has organic, animal beauty; but so wholly is this part of his nature overshadowed by his higher endowments, that no mere flush and fulness of physical life can meet or fill our idea of beauty in man.

The human body is not simply a living body, but the soul's instrument: the face is not merely the seat of all surface senses, but a translucency in whose shadows come and go the reflections of a spiritual life. The symbols of thought and signs of feeling which are found in man and in man's action, to be at all apprehended, must, therefore, be understood in their relation to the superior spiritual powers and duties which lie back of them. No cheap excellency of color and form, of grace and courtesy, is permitted unto man. Much has been given unto him, and much must be required.

of him. Mere delicacy and symmetry of features, if not displeasing, have little power to arrest the attention, and none to refresh the heart.

What is highest in man must be discovered, and this must rule out that which is base and overrule that which is inferior. Anything in feature or act which reveals a lower impulse triumphing over a higher, and which so presents itself to the spectator, cannot be deemed pleasing, cannot be deemed beautiful. A work must be commendable and noble before it can be beautiful, and that which speaks of degradation and bondage must, to every mind attuned to health and freedom, be painful. We are not prepared for a high ideal of manly beauty till we possess a high idea of man, — till, having brought him up in the worth of character, we show him in feature and act for that which he is. We need not stop to insist, that to enthrone the physical in man, either in the baser form of a rounded and lusty contour, or in the nobler form of bone and sinew, is to overlook the spiritual, — to sink it in the simply organic, — is to make men, not a little lower than the angels, but a little higher than the brutes, — is, not to establish the divine in the flesh, but to smother the divine with the flesh, — is to extinguish the torch which, burning behind the tracery, reveals its divine pattern.

Nor is the danger less certain, though less extreme, in regarding man as pure intellect, — in watching and striving to trace only the workings of thought. The larger share of life is not in thinking, but in feeling; the better share of life, not in right thinking, but in right feeling. It is not truth latent in thought, but patent in the character, — truth passing into the heart, and thence, through the will, into that only great product of man, conduct, — that gives pleasure. Man may not only think the truth, but feel it, and build himself upon it; and these his higher prerogatives we demand shall in some form or other be brought out before we accord the praise of spiritual beauty. That which is highest in man is a loving apprehension of the true and the right, and that which is highest in conduct is the victory of these over error and wrong. That, then, gives us pleasure in man as man, which is the mark of a spirit loyal to truth and right. Treachery and desertion here are a meanness for which, if truly understood, nothing can atone. In these two intuitions is discerned the progress of the creative plan in man, and we insist that there should be no regression. That in expression which conceives and realizes this progress is the basis of spiritual beauty; that is, beauty resting on spiritual qualities. He only who apprehends strongly and clearly the new type of creation furnished in man, and what, therefore, is to be looked for in a being lifted within the realm of truth and right, can either fully understand or powerfully present the signs of manly character, and thus of manly beauty. As in the inorganic and organic kingdoms, the line of beauty runs parallel with that of order and creation, so here we have a new spiritual creation, and a new spiritual order is demanded.

Before, weakness, decay, and death were the deforming agents; but here ignorance, — for ignorance is the weakness of this realm, — error, and vice are these agents, and on whatever these put their seal, there is seen that discomfiture of reason, that defeat of virtue, which is true deformity.

In the beauty which belongs to man, lower organic

beauty is included, gathered up as an element, yet a secondary and feeble element, with that which is broader, fuller, and nobler. That expression which Ruskin terms the appearance of felicitous fulfilment of function in living things may still be present, but is no longer first or second in importance, and is modified and overborne by the temper of the spiritual and intellectual life.

Not chiefly, however, does the human body claim to be recognized in its own beauties, but much more imperatively in its own rights. It may show service strongly and freely rendered, but not service exacted in ascetic rigor. By far the most painful expression in man is that which shows a servant enthroned, the license and debauchery of appetite, the malignity of insane passion, the whole man put to vile and wicked uses. This is a temple desecrated, — an altar with an impure sacrifice, — violence in the seat of mercy. Only secondary to this is the rigor of asceticism, finding a grim pleasure in the waste and squalor it has created. Though a despotic and harsh rule of mind over body can never so repel us as the usurped dominion of the unclean lusts, — harpies of the flesh, — yet both imply an intestine and most unhappy warfare, in which victory on either side is the pillage and devastation of a portion of man's inheritance. To the mind that understands these signs of a civil, a domestic feud, they must be disagreeable. Guarding against the one danger, we say that the body should show service performed, not government by it exercised. The steed, though foaming, must be reined, and not a runaway. The mind must animate, pleasurably animate, and powerfully control every member and feature of the body. Faithful service, fidelity, is the body's highest honor, and it must know and make known that it is the pliant instrument of an honored master.

Guarding against the other danger, we say the body may show use, but not abuse. Self-torture is not to be disguised under the name of self-rule, nor is it to be hinted that there is a necessary and radical hostility between the constituents of man's nature. The physical is not to be the victim of the spiritual, the body is not to be burned out or dissolved away in the laboratory of thought. It is not over the decay and ashes of organic structure that mind is to reign, but over its most perfected product, nor alone over it, but in it and with it, finding often the measure of its own strength in that of its physical instrument.

In seeking, therefore, for that expression in man which is the basis of beauty, the body must be regarded, not as a living thing simply, but as, in all its complex functions, the organ of spirit, and in it there must be sought the signs of perfect and felicitous control by an agent itself in spiritual health. That which is unhealthy in the mind or in its action on the body cannot, so far as discerned, give the impression of beauty. It is regression and failure, weighing us down with a sense of defeat.

A fact comes in here, however, which must always greatly modify our views of that which is beautiful in the world and in man, — the fact of sin. The spirit is in a real, though not a necessary and inherent, conflict with the body, or, as we now designate it, the flesh. The virtue, and therefore the beauty of man, ceases to be the virtue of repose. There are necessarily in him, when most victorious, traces of the battle, and we are no longer displeased, therefore, with that which shows the subtile, strong workings of evil, if only it is evil subdued.

We shall mark the effect on taste of this knowledge of conflict in human virtue in several directions.

(*a.*) The body is suffered to show marks of severity, to bear visible traces of its crucifixion under the spirit, and this, because we all know it a restive and treacherous servant.

As we have seen its guilt, we are not startled or offended by its manacles. Though still withdrawing from angelic and perfect natures any appearance of struggle, we yet know that struggle is and must be present in man, and are not displeased with evidences in the body of stern discipline and unceasing rule. It is remembered that victory is always to the defeated severity, and in the pale and attenuated features there is a willingness to see the triumph of a better impulse. Every human face is searched for traces of the conflict, and we expect there something of the stern regimen of the battle-field. Great scope is here given amid the shifting phases of passion for the development of partial good, of power regained, though not held with the repose of untempted virtue.

(*b.*) As a result of this conflict, strength, and even sternness of will, are sought in expression. As man's career is or should be a prolonged resistance, a persistent toil, as crime and obstacles are to be surmounted, temptations to be overcome, and dangers to be met, nothing but will can take a firm stand or push a determined advance. We often recognize, therefore, with pleasure, in human expression that which is rough and rugged, that which is firm and forcible, since in these virtue may find a citadel and guilt a retribution. So conscious is man every moment of the need of strength, and, above all, of the strength which can say no to passion, that will is ever felt to be the very framework of character, and we care not if it occasionally lie on the surface in massive ribbed strength.

(*c.*) This sense of a present and most urgent struggle makes us less content than ever with simple intellect in expression. We demand that every man should take a part, and show the right part which he has taken in this conflict.

Our distrust and fear of men, the dangerous depths of the race lie in feeling, in passion, and in purpose; and no one stands revealed in the manner of his manhood, till revealed at these points. We wish, therefore, to see the breaking out of character, — the utterance, not of truth merely, but of one's heart toward the truth. Pure thinking is a disguise, — an abstraction; we wish to see the disclosed, — the concrete man as he is and feels.

(*d.*) A sense of the sternness of the conflict between rule and anarchy — between right and wayward tendencies in man — makes every, even the slightest indications, and those too of a partial victory, pleasurable. Symmetrical and stalwart virtue is too much to be often anticipated, and the feeble appearance of single graces, like the putting forth of early flowers amid frosts and snow, brings pleasure. It is the hard rule of winter which gives to the spring a loveliness, not lost even when contrasted with the luxuriance of the later season. It is the desert desolation of a sordid and selfish heart that imparts such grace to all human virtue, and makes it more rare and enviable than angelic excellence. This acceptance which feeble and partial things find in man greatly increases the variety of expression, and thus of beauty found in character. If ideal perfection were in each instance requisite, character must soon cease to include that which was new, to modify or exclude that which was old. Every happy stroke and correct delineation would be a new limitation from which we could not depart, and our perfection would be lost in the monotony of its own excellence. The infinite may be unchangeable, and, as ever eluding the grasp of man, preserve its scope. The finite, made unchangeable, dies at once, and, fortunately, in the very weakness of its perceptions and powers, finds a reason for that infinite variety which is nevertheless infinite deficiency.

(*e.*) Another result of the known and universal presence of evil is, that in a complex whole characters of unmitigated meanness or malice are suffered to appear. As no pain is given by those signs which in the individual indicate a temptation, if it be a temptation resisted, — a passion, if it be a passion ruled, — so, in the group, a Shylock or an Iago may be present, if Shylock be baffled and self-tortured, and if to Iago there "remains the censure of a hellish villain."

Evil, which in the individual stood represented by an untamed impulse, in the drama and novel, presenting a more formidable and compact power, takes possession of its agents, and through them pushes to the quick the champions and martyrs of virtue. As the field is broader, the sin is broader, and marshals its own distinct forces. While, therefore, we still may take no pleasure in villany as villany, yet, as vanquished villany, as that which has raised virtue into valor, it plays a most essential part, — makes life soul-stirring and tragic, and is the dark, retreating cloud along whose gilded edges the now dominant light shows all its brilliancy. Avarice, envy, and malice are not less deformed and deforming; but we need the contrast of their depths, to give height to our virtue, — the strength of the evil, to measure the power of that good which has subdued it.

The same principle, however, applies to the group and the narrative as to the portrait and the biography. The preponderance — the settling of the scales, both of justice and of power — must be with virtue, — must so be as to mark the presence of a true and irresistible spiritual power. Otherwise, our better impulses, baffled and deserted, fall back in despair on themselves, or rise up to reject the lie. Treason and the halter, villany and judgment, are as consonant as fidelity and success, courage and victory. Whatever may be the transient relation of things, we have patience to wait, if the issues indicate that there is power with truth, and that there is a growth into moral order, though the foundations of that order be laid in the hard, unchipped granite of justice.

It is evident, with the perverted and shifting sense of right which belongs to men, there will be endless variety in what they will term beautiful. They may choose, in the play or the painting, to overlook leading tendencies and radical issues, to fix the attention on minor points, and, on the basis of these, to pronounce the work beautiful. They may refuse to see a portion of the expression, and, exalting another portion, distort their judgment; or, incapable of discovering the undercurrent of truth, of understanding the combined voice of the whole, the parts may be a dull or melancholy medley. But where there is no concealment, and no distortion through a limited or perverted perception, it is evident the healthy heart will only receive pleasure from that expression which is healthy, and that the false, the morbid, the faithless, can never be to it the basis of beauty. Each of these imply a spiritual disease, and when distinctly seen produce the impression of deformity or ugliness. A man's estimates of beauty in the moral world can neither pass much beyond or fall much below his virtue. It is this which indicates his apprehension of the relations, the law, the order, the inferiority and superiority, the better and the worse, which belong to spirit, and hence of the excellency which is possible to it. But this, his judgment of virtue, once shaped, the beauty of all action is thereby determined, and the mind refuses to take pleasure in that which to it indicates weakness and a failure of thought and spirit, — the very energies whose action was to be displayed.

(*f.*) It also results from the presence of evil, that we take pleasure in the manifestation of certain emotions, which are in themselves painful, and indicate a desertion of right impulses, such as remorse and shame. These are the last efforts of defeated virtue, the pulsations which indicate the presence of life and the possibility of its return. They come in, therefore, to redeem the terror of a death which otherwise hastens to be perfect. Remorse ought to be, shame ought to be, and we are glad to see that this last law which remains to guilt is unbroken. In the sad though not unkind climate of this world, shame and penitence have a renewing, fructifying power, are themselves the bursting bud of virtue. Pity and sadness are gentler emotions in the same manner begotten and justified by the fact of evil. Every man quick in his perception and sensitive in his feelings, must find an only too frequent occasion for them, and whenever, therefore, rightly expressed, they will kindle the subdued pleasure of sympathy. Even the grief of virtue has in it a tincture of joy.

As the fruit of this discussion, we say that, in this human world, that expression alone will be to any mind beautiful which indicates to it the felicitous action of the powers at work; that the notion of what constitutes success must vary greatly with the intelligence and virtue of the beholder; and that a sense of conflict and resistance modifies all our judgments.

It was to be expected that more pleasure should be felt in organic than in inorganic beauty, and in human beauty than in either, since here is the higher work, the fuller expression, the more immediate and personal interests. So true is this, that what has been said of beauty in the fields of physical and vital forces would be but a very partial presentation, were we not now to trace the reflex action of human feeling on all that nature presents. Though the rock and the lichen, the mountain and the forest, are valued for what they intrinsically contain, they often have a much higher power from a certain sympathy which is established between them and man, by which he does not so much receive what they nakedly present as invest them with some of his own attributes and relations, and cause them to reflect his own feelings. Not that nature is a simple sounding-board to the soul of man, sending back to him anything he may choose to utter, but that, through the eager interpretation of his own heart, he is able to discover in her something of the same conflict which he experiences in himself, — to rejoice in the achievements of her productive power as a triumph, to mourn over her failure and decay as a new breaking out of the serpent virus, to feel the hope of her smile and the life of her summer, the dejection of her frown and the despair of her bitter cold.

Owing to this shadowing forth of his own states in the states of nature, many things give pleasure to man which would otherwise have no power to gratify.

(*a.*) Power simply destructive, like that of the earthquake and tornado, and apparently including a violent regression, may still excite the feeling of sublimity. Thoroughly conscious of his own weakness and of the necessity of power as the basis of all good, nothing moves man more deeply than its manifestations; most pleasurably as well as most profoundly when it is power in the service of creative wisdom and love; yet profoundly when, wild and wayward, it seems for the moment the breaking out of superabundant and unconstrained strength. When the spectator is not pressed into terror by the too immediate presence of a dangerous agency, its action does not rest upon the mind simply as wilful, cruel destruction, only the more inexplicable and horrible as it is the more extended. If this were its impression, the sense of power would be overruled, as in the merciless sack of a city, and the only feeling excited would be that of horror.

More often, the mind either looks beyond its apparent or immediate effects, as in the case of the storm, and feels, amid all its wrath, the presence of a remedial agency; or it sees in it the image of justice, and, clothing it with retribution, finds its sense of moral order met; or, it regards this work of devastation as the finishing up and sweeping away of the old, about to give place to the new. In all these cases, the feeling of power is left to operate upon the soul, and work therein its own sense of elevation. Those agencies, however, which speak a language of pure violence, of retreat and ruin, can only terrify and repel.

(*b.*) Scenes of desolation, worn and wasted, which, for their physical and organic expression, would not be beautiful, may nevertheless be so through their relation to man, — their expression of moral truth. The ruined city, amid the heaping sands of the desert, may be a most forcible utterance of the liabilities, — the transient character of human work, — of the fate, the issues, of nature as locked up in, and subordinate to, those of man.

We have already seen how abundant and ever-present in man is the wild, the dark, and the sad; and these, by an inevitable sympathy, will draw with them that which is wild, dark, and sad in nature. The courage of our mariners, the endurance of our heroes, the faith of our explorers, must be measured by severe tests, and these will be found in the angry ocean, the relentless desert, and inexorable polar ice. There must be the rock and cavern for the hermit and saint of sackcloth, the wilderness for the prophet with camel's hair and leathern girdle. In fine, as man's scale of healthy feeling ranges from exultant joy to sadness, from the quick and merry peal of pleasure to those deeper, slower chords which would have never been strung but for sin, — there must be in that nature which is to enter in as a subdued and harmonized chorus, — which is to make the whole a concord, — the same variety of emotion. Thus is it that the unfinished and waste places of nature, her weakness, and the decay of her organic structures, may often be as expressive as what was before termed her felicitous fulfilment of living functions.

(*c.*) We before saw that variety in man implied a deficiency, which yet, through our sense of his finiteness, gave no offence. We shall also accept and rejoice in much in the world about us, which, viewed from one point, might indicate desertion and unfinished work. The rock-ribbed mountain, though rent, rugged, and barren, rightly stands over against the exuberant life of the valley, for there is in it another line of action, — a new record of power, and a sterner sense of conflict. It is not in the towering forest alone that we delight, but in the feebler, but not less perfect, victory of the violet.

(*d.*) What we may term our ideal of any plant or animal is, by this sympathy of men with effort and a mission fulfilled, greatly modified. It is not always the tree that is most luxuriant, nor the flower which is largest and most complete, which has the most power over the heart. The tree which, in the very track of storms, stands furthest out on the lean soil of sterile rocks, the forlorn hope of the vegetable kingdom, may move us more than the indolent, glutted occupant of the meadow. The delicate dwarfed flower that has earliest felt the touch of spring, and, first to escape the yielding winter, has crept from amid the snows, a weak but joyful harbinger of the yet distant summer, has a voice of watching and hope not to be heard again from all the loitering ranks of spring or autumn.

Says Ruskin: "The first time that I saw the *Soldanella Alpina* before spoken of, it was growing of magnificent size on a sunny Alpine pasture among bleating of sheep and lowing of cattle associated with a pro fusion of *Geum montanum* and *Ranunculus Pyrenæus.* I noticed it only because new to me, nor perceived any peculiar beauty in its cloven flower. Some days after, I found it alone among the rack of the higher clouds and howling of glacier-winds, and, as I descried it, piercing through an edge of avalanche, which, in its retiring, had left the new ground brown and lifeless, and as if burned by recent fire; the plant was poor and feeble, and seemingly exhausted with its efforts, but it was then that I comprehended its ideal character, and saw its noble function and order of glory among the constellations of the earth.

"The *Ranunculus glacialis* might perhaps by cultivation be blanched from its wan and corpse-like paleness to purer white, and won to more branched and lofty development of its ragged leaves. But the ideal of the plant is to be found only in the last loose stones of the moraine, alone there; wet with the cold, unkindly drip of the glacier-water, and trembling as the loose and steep dust to which it clings yields ever and anon, and shudders and crumbles away from about its roots."

Something allied to this is seen in our estimate of the coarser and more strongly-colored flowers of Fall. The aster and the golden-rod will, when compared with the spring-beauty and the early anemone, hardly bear the plucking. But the position assigned them is very different; and, standing where nature placed them, amid the rougher, bolder work of autumn, the full-grown grass, the rank weeds, and the reddening shrubbery, they greatly enrich the scene and make gorgeous the decadence of the year.

The discovery of a place occupied, an office performed, is felt to be a new pleasure in any object.

(*e.*) The most important reflex action of the nature

of man on the nature below it is that by which a moral quality is widely imparted to beauty. We wish, not only to see thought and skill, but these employed in the ministration of love. Sensitive organism, to be beautiful, must ever by its action secure its own pleasure. The happiness, the good of the thing created must present itself as habitually and perseveringly included in the creative plan. Thus, the moral character of the Creator stands revealed in his work, and the mind seeks for, and chiefly delights in, that revelation, as we before saw it to delight in the open and healthy action of man's moral nature. It is never forgotten that benevolence should pre-eminently belong to God, and that the love which enters into his creation and providence, showing him everywhere the only untiring benefactor, is our best hope and promise. The mind taught in the region of human action looks on everything as a disclosure of character on the part of the Divine agent whose work it is, and thus directly transfers to every beautiful as to every excellent object a feeling, — the feeling which in the heart of God gave rise to it, and shaped it. No wise action is without its end, its significance, its moral quality.

The first thing which we have now pointed out as the basis of beauty, as the substance in which it inheres, is expression. This expression has also been defined in the inorganic world as the manifest presence of a creative, formative thought, — as advancing truth; in the organic world, as the successful and the pleasurable fulfilment of vital functions, — as advancing life, which also is the advance of higher truth; in the rational world, as the acceptance of the law of reason, the advance, the victory, of the right, and this, too, in the midst of conflict.

LECTURE IV.

SECOND CONDITION OF BEAUTY, UNITY.—UNITY AND VARIETY EXPLAINED.—SUBLIMITY.—ABSOLUTE AND RELATIVE BEAUTY.

BEAUTY is not a primary, direct quality of things. There are not certain things to the exclusion of others which have this as a property, as some fluids are corrosive and some volatile. This quality may be gained or lost by an object with each change of arrangement in its parts. It is not inherent in the thing, but belongs to the aptness and power of the thing in its present form or present office. It is not a constituent of the matter making a rose, but arises from the transient relation and expression which that matter has assumed. Virtue is not a quality of all action nor of the same action in all circumstances, but only of actions which stand in a certain relation to the person performing them and the persons affected by them. In like manner, the lower virtue of beauty is taken up and lost with the expression in which it inheres. Expression we have therefore given as the first condition in the object of beauty, — as that in things and actions which gives rise as a cause to beauty,—which furnishes the true substance of which beauty is a quality. A second condition of beauty is unity, or, as expressed on both sides, unity and variety. This is not something in addition to the expression, but is the method of the expression,—the form which utterance assumes. Expression is found in the beautiful object, and found there under the form of unity. The object, that it may be beautiful, is conditioned to expression; the expression is conditioned to unity.

Unity is one of the most widely recognized criterions of beauty, and has sometimes been confounded with that to which it so often gives rise.

But the unity of a thing is to the mind a wholly distinct and separable quality from its beauty, and will not be found necessarily to include, or uniformly to involve, the rarer, richer attribute. The general recognition, however, of unity in all distinctively beautiful objects, while failing to show its identity with the higher expression, yet helps to mark it as an antecedent, a condition thereof.

The unity to which reference is now had is not that of office, as the concurrence of wheels in a machine, nor is it the unity of mere existence in the same place or time, but the harmony of expression by which the parts of an object unite in producing and deepening a single feeling. It is a harmony of emotions, as music is a harmony of sounds, and implies no direct resemblance, much less sameness, in the objects between which it exists, in the means by which it is produced. Unity implies plurality, variety, and designates that concurrent power of the parts by which they become in their action on the mind a whole, lending themselves to a single effect. The absolute unit, — the one, — cannot be the source of beauty, for it has in it no obvious revelation of thought or feeling. It includes no relation, and as contemplated alone stands in no relation.

The mind of man does not penetrate essences, does not perceive power or wisdom in simple existence; it is only in the mode and relations of that existence that he discovers these. It is the correspondence and ministration of parts, the presence of an office or function, and the ability to meet that function; the compacting of various members into symmetrical wholes; the obvious reference of each thing to something without itself, called an end; a relating and ordering in reference to each other of things which exist, — that mark for man the presence of thought.

We must go, therefore, beyond the unit before we have anything fitted to reveal a plan, a purpose, a power, to the intellect, and thus move the feelings.

Indeed, long before our analysis reaches the final unit, things become too barren of relation to make the impression of beauty. A straight line, a limited section of the most graceful curve, a single color, though each letters in the alphabet of beauty, as yet uncompounded into intelligible expression, teach nothing and secure nothing. A fine pigment that lies unshapen on the palette impresses the eye, but not the intellect; it is brilliant, but not beautiful: transferred to the canvas, it assumes form, relation, office, and entering the region of thought, may now claim for itself a rational attribute, — beauty.

Since, therefore, thought is brought out in relations, and not in naked existence, we must have these relations — that is, plurality, variety — before we can have any strictly rational feeling. Some degree of complexity is the indispensable condition of thought, and of those emotions which spring, not from perception, but apprehension.

Beauty, truth, and right inhere in objects, propositions, and actions, not directly as qualities inhere in things, but in them as subjects of thought: the statue is thought to be beautiful; the proposition is thought to be true; the action is thought to be right. But each of the three as subjects of thought are complex. Thought cannot act on the single, but only on the plural; its first product, a judgment, implies at least two conceptions. As beauty does not arise from a sensation whose content is a thing, but from an intellection whose content is a thought, and as a thought must contain more than one element, beauty can never be found in the absolute unit: variety is its perpetual condition. Only in a relation, a combination of parts, is found that expression which is its basis.

On the other hand, the variety cannot be an unharmonized and discordant variety. Otherwise, the mind, unable to reconcile the members in any connection, to contemplate them as one, is forced back upon the parts, and the variety which it seemed to have obtained is again lost. Each fragment still stands alone, a stone in a yet unerected building, and makes only its single impression. It is by the concurrent, and not the conflicting, action of various things, that the mind receives a more powerful impulse than belonged to any of the parts.

We have now, not a unit, but a unity. The first is single in itself, and single in its impression on the senses; the second is complex in its elements, and complex in its sensuous impression, but one in its action on mind. The band of thought has gathered the fagots into a bundle. The plan of the architect has led us to overlook the individual stones in the individual building. This synthesis is, and is felt to be, the triumph of concordant thought over discordant matter, and in the extent and perfection of this triumph are found the degrees of beauty. It does not merely aggregate the power already present in the parts, but establishes a new relation therein, creates a new power not before existent. Paints pass into paintings, sounds into music, acts into achievements, and words into character.

Beauty, then, demands variety in its object, since thus only can there be combination, expression: it demands unity, since thus only is there combination, thus only is the sensible made the intellectual, and the diversity of things the harmony of thought. The unity is supplied from within, the diversity is found without in facts and objects, and the relation of these two elements we need to unfold in several directions.

(*a.*) The variety may often be striking and startling without at all disturbing the oneness of expression. The power of the thought is seen in its command of full and diverse expression.

As the unity now spoken of is only a unity of the mind's imparting and the mind's receiving, it is evident that it is not exclusively dependent upon, nor does it certainly follow, any form of external unity. It may consist with resemblance, and it may still more markedly consist with certain forms of diversity. Contrast may carry feeling to its highest intensity; on this condition, however, that it does not become a conflict of opposite emotions. The predominating feeling of any work must have no rival, and yet it may make a foil of adverse emotions, and thereby itself be more distinctly felt. The garden that includes no waste within its own walls, may yet make us the more sensible of its wealth by the wild without it. Power finds a simultaneous and double expression in the rest of the rocky shore, and in the unceasing, impetuous motion of the waves that dash upon it. Repose is imaged as plainly in the silent mountains uplifted against the sky, as in the sheltered valleys at their base ; fear and despair are as clearly set forth in the last thin beams of a winter sun, as in the cold, dun clouds and unyielding night which extinguish them. The deformed beggars gathered at the beautiful gate of the temple give in brighter relief the physical and spiritual power of the Apostles. The courageous, unhesitating faith of a leader is seen, not less in the fickle, fearful emotions of those about him, than in his own repose and strength. Nature has not only many thoughts, but many and most diverse methods of uttering the same thought, and a free and powerful variety will hold these at command. Witnesses to the same truth will come up from opposite sides and from remote kingdoms. It will not be the power of objects over the senses, but their power over the intellect, that will assign them their position, and the latter will sometimes take pleasure in the bold manner in which she overrules and contradicts the former.

Cause and effect constitute the most stern of all the connections in the external world ; and, as containing for the mind more of truth than any other, will most constantly appear as a controlling principle amid all variety. That which is a law of thought and order elsewhere, though present in beauty in a less strict and obtrusive form, will yet give direction and limitation to every force. Our variety will not be a mere fortuity, a chance-medley, but will everywhere show the surf-marks of great natural forces. It will be suggestive of what has preceded it, what is to come after it, and show where it takes hold on things that are. And yet the variety of beauty is not bound down to philosophy or natural science.

Art, while heeding science, is constantly transcending it. No complex series of causes, even in the physical world, is so well understood as not to leave most of its hourly phenomena inexplicable. Form, feature, color, method, the things wherein expression lurks, are in their details capable of very little critical knowledge, and receive but a very general law from science. We know something of the type, the generic form, but very little of the many individual forms under which it may appear. The painter does not find himself straitened in the variety of his plants and animals by observing the most accurate classifications of botany and zoölogy. The intuitive power of the reason is left without the guidance of science in its efforts to apprehend the symbols of life, and so to combine these, that they shall freely utter what it would have them utter. It is not the rough work, the meagre outline, explained by known causes, and reached by tracing these in their effects, that give beauty, but the faithful presentation of forces doing a perfect work, — but how doing it we know not. In every department, experience gives us much in sensible properties and associations merely; much, therefore, which art uses with but a very limited reference to science.

The regions of fancy also stretch beyond those of fact, and though the two territories ever so skirt the one upon the other as to establish a sympathy of laws and manners, yet each more wayward dream of the creative mind can spring up yonder under milder criticism as in a land not explored or mapped. When we add to this the fact, that in rational life there is recognized a free-will much less calculable in its results than cause, — a supernatural element with ever widening relations,—we shall see at once, that the variety, both in nature and art, which is the basis of beauty, is not straitened by science; that sculpture is in no danger of becoming a branch of physiology, music of acoustics, or poetry of philosophy. The most rigid stratification is liable to a fault, clouds do not always guarantee a storm, nor the beginning of life forecast its end.

Knowledge, in its rapid advancement, far from crippling, becomes a convenient law to the imagination, making it more chaste, truthful, and rational, and itself assigning form and meaning to much which would otherwise be to art formless and meaningless. A wider recognition of truth, far from restricting beauty, fills the world with new and marvellous suggestions, and makes the little that is known, amid the much that remains unknown, most quickening to the imagination, declarative of a most subtile and pervasive power. The truths of cause and effect, of science rarely limiting variety, will often unite, in most compact and powerful expression, things before thought too diverse or accidental for any convergence. We are in danger of knowing, not too much, but too little, for the highest impression of objects. The unknown is to the mind the confused, the chaotic; and only as knowledge moves through it revealing thought, plan, expression, can beauty follow, taking possession of it as a conquered realm.

(*b.*) The unity in which variety is contained is not always equally strict. It is true, that the power of the expression must depend on the singleness of the thought which links the parts, and its entire control of each of them; but much that is beautiful is rather a harmony of many pleasant impressions, than a compact, forcible rendering of a single expression.

The unity secured is oftener that of the genus than of the species. The landscape contains a thousand pleasing things: more rarely it combines them, subordinating part to part in a single unique and vigorous expression. The mind seeks after, and takes an especial delight in, the higher, stricter unity of one governing element, but gratefully accepts a concord of agreeable things. In proportion as the space decreases, and the things presented become fewer, the mind claims an increase of unity, and this for three reasons. It seems more readily secured. Some of the objects in a wide field may be more restive, more stubbornly diverse; but as these diminish, the ease with which a uniting thought is found increases. The very fact also of this narrowness, this singleness of the group, seems to imply that all parts must share common circumstances and impulses. If the group is one of men, and passion is present, it must be the same for all; if of plants, the conditions of life must be alike to all. A third reason is, that, in proportion as things partially diverse are crowded together, the diversity is made more apparent, and creates in the mind either the conflict of opposites or the confusion of the unarranged. A series of paintings may do what one cannot be made to do. A park may contain what cannot in miniature be successfully represented in a garden.

(*c.*) Nature, amid an illimitable variety, preserves the unity of her work by a constant repetition, under specific differences, of generic forms and colors; under individual differences, of specific forms and colors. The basis of her beauty and her science is the same. That which is classification to the intellect is harmony and rhythm to the emotions. As unity has two conditions, agreement and differences, it has also two opposite dangers, sameness and confusion; the monotony of identical forms mechanically repeated, the disorder of variable forms endlessly shifted. Between these, nature preserves her safe path, never leaving her parts involved beyond the mind's grasp in the chaos of materials and elements, nor yet reducing them to block and brick work, to dead surfaces and unbroken angles. Each species of tree has its own typical form, involving, with much variety, so many, and such undistinguishable things as to escape description, and yet returning with so much uniformity to certain lines and relations, as never to escape the disciplined eye. With or without foliage, near by or remote, the ash, the maple, the linden, reveal themselves, and yet leave the mind unable to explain the certainty of its own conviction. So, also, is it with the relation of fibres in the several kinds of wood. Small fragments, when cut in different methods, and from different portions of the tree, disclose amid themselves a great variety of surface, yet all of them have the indefinable additional stamp of their species. The leaf repeats the specific, but never the individual form. The bough, while branching in obedience to the life of the tree, also has a peculiar office to fulfil. The tree, while knowing and feeling the method of its class, remembers also the new conditions under which the old problem is to be solved, and grows up as distinct and individual as if it were the only representative of the tribe. The forest, while gathering into its ranks trees in all their varieties, disposes the several kinds so sparingly, so in reference to each other, and by resemblance of habits, as never to confound the mind or suffer the wealth of its resources to degenerate into prodigality.

It never wastes, in the wantonness of the hour, that reserved power by which wood and forest are distinguished from each other, and made new chapters in the vegetable kingdom. A similar sameness and variety of forms are traceable in hills and mountains, and thus in the landscape of which these are controlling features.

What has now been illustrated in form may be seen in color in the plumage of birds. So numerous are birds, so little accessible to the senses, so migratory in their habits, that here, especially, is variety liable to lapse into confusion. Proportionately decided and firm is the principle by which unity is preserved. We have exactness of color as well as exactness of form. The individual does, indeed, within the limits of the species find minor shades of difference, but these limits are carefully marked and watchfully guarded. Color, though of great variety and richness of pattern, with many most elaborate and specific markings, is no longer that vacillating thing we often find it elsewhere, but becomes a most obvious and unmistakable mark of the class, and thus of the habits and character, of the bird. Without this mark, all would become confusion, even to the more careful student; with it, all is order to the comparatively careless observer. In domestic fowls, where no such danger of confounding species exists, this principle of unity is relaxed, and variety is enlarged through every shade and combination of colors. The variety of individuals, when it would endanger, to the eye at least, the distinction of species, is restricted, and its place supplied by a most marked variety of species firmly preserved. When, however, the species is unmistakable, as in the dove and the hen, and sameness is ready to become an unmeaning monotony, color ceases to be stable, and, from black to white, from red to violet, ranges through the spectrum.

(*d.*) We have reserved till now the distinction between beauty, grandeur, and sublimity, since it can be best considered in connection with unity and variety. These three are but distinctions under the generic term beauty; certain more marked and peculiar forms of beauty being distinguished by the names grandeur and sublimity. That beauty and sublimity are but two extremes, the lower and higher manifestations of the same qualities, is evident from many examples. The peacefully flowing river is beautiful; as it gathers impulse and purpose, and rushes on in rapids it becomes grand; when, shivered and wild with motion, it leaps the cataract in eager masses, it is sublime. By an imperceptible transition and growth of expression, we have passed from simple beauty to sublimity. An increase of dimensions imparts grandeur in architecture, and the stretch of even a naked desert may impress us with a kindred feeling. A character shaped upon truth is beautiful; standing upon truth amid the violence of enemies, is grand; adhering to truth amid the derision of friends, and in defiance of the rack and the fagot, is sublime. It is usually said that power is the essential expression of all sublime objects. To make this true, the word must include much more than mere physical power. Duration, magnitude, any beautiful expression which enlarges and overpowers the mind in its apprehension, may become sublime. It is the fulness and force of the expression always implying power, and often its direct utterance, that excite this more intense and elevated emotion. Strictly speaking, there are three directions in which the mind may be outstripped by the expression: in space, which is magnitude; in time, which is duration; in intensity, which is power; and these will together or independently give rise to the sublime.

In a sublime object the unity of the expression is great, and also the variety. There is no doubt or division in the impression, though it arises from so many points, and so intensely from each that the mind is unable to estimate it. The variety, though united to our apprehension and feeling, escapes the judgment, and leaves the mind overpowered by the sense of its fulness. Arithmetic is vanquished, and power as an unmeasured magnitude presses upon the feelings. As long as the sources of expression are calculable and measurable, the mind remains in a more quiet and composed attitude, but when it is sensible that these are escaping it, are overwhelming it, that it is in the midst of that which bespeaks the unmeasured and the infinite, it is lifted up, and, according to the original force of the word, becomes sublime. The impression of the sublime, then, is due to the escape of variety, though in connection with the most intense unity, from the judgment, the mind's measurements.

There are several considerations which tend to establish this view. In a tranquil ocean, there is great sameness of parts, and we do not receive the impression of sublimity from a limited surface. Ten acres or a square mile of ocean has no hold upon the heart. It is only when the sky dips to the water, and the two pass out together, that the mind falters in its pursuit, and is made to feel how all things elude its senses. Here the variety which the judgment has not estimated is made up of an endless repetition of similar parts, and the extent must be all the greater in proportion as this sameness aids the mind's action. A desert farm is one thing; a desert continent quite another.

On the other hand, when the ocean is wakeful to the winds, and every foot of surface is a shifting and perpetual strife, shrouded in its own spray of battle, the mind is easily overtasked, and a narrow vista opened through the mist gives it more than it can apprehend. Here, the variety, having more of diversity, readily escapes the apprehension, and, in a comparatively limited field, produces the impression of sublimity.

It has been found that order is sometimes favorable to the sublime; at other times, disorder. An army produces the impression by its order; the mountain range by its disorder, — its traces of volcanic action. This similarity of effects from apparently opposite causes is yet due to the same principle. It is only the aggregate movement of men that can have in it so much power as to startle the mind. Order here, therefore, serves to intensify and bring out the expression, and is thus its only hope of sublimity; without order, the mind is left to contemplate individuals; with order, it contemplates an army.

On the other hand, confusion and disorder amid the elements of nature, regarded as all obedient to one force, disturb the mind in its estimate of that force, and cause it to be more readily overpowered with a sense of magnitude. In the one case, the parts are distinct, and it is only by their combination in so large a whole as to tax the apprehension, that they can reach sublimity. In the other, all objects are under the dominion of one force, and this eludes us the more readily by the irregularity of its action. The sublime is aided in two directions, either by that which multiplies the power, — this order sometimes does; or by that which embarrasses the mind in its apprehension of that power, — this confusion and darkness frequently do. In either case, the principle is the same, — a multiplication of parts either in sameness or diversity escaping the mind's estimates. It should be remembered, that in the expression variety and unity, variety may sometimes mean nothing more than multiplicity, — a repetition of similar parts.

(*e.*) There remains another distinction often made, and best discussed in this connection; that of absolute and relative beauty. Some things are spoken of as absolutely beautiful, — beautiful in themselves; others, as relatively beautiful, — beautiful in their connections with other objects. This distinction does not seem to be well taken. All beauty is a beauty of relations of parts gathered into a whole. We may subdivide the object under consideration, and make of it several distinct objects, or unite it with others and make of it a still more complex object. But, in each case, the object, whether a landscape, a tree in the landscape, or a flower on the tree, is beautiful or otherwise through the relation of its parts. Each object, the flower, the tree, the landscape, is complex, containing members, and also as a member is included in that which is higher. When I pronounce the flower beautiful, but the tree, of which it is a part, deformed, there is no conflict in my judgments. In each it is a question of relations, and while the right relations are found in the one object, they are not found in the other. The awkward position of the flower on the tree is a question of the beauty of the tree, and not of the flower. Many objects are complex, including parts distinct and complete in themselves, and these yet other parts. If we start with the simplest whole, and pass up to the most inclusive whole, we shall find a series of distinct questions propounded, each involving new principles of arrangement, and capable of a distinct answer. From lowest to highest, however, all is relative beauty, if we understand by this expression the beauty of relations; all, absolute, intrinsic beauty, if we understand by this a beauty in its conditions wholly interior to the object considered. There is another class of objects, of which the parts are not all of them complete in themselves, but dependent on their combination for expression. Such are some of the members of a building. These are not wholes, and have no beauty save as parts of a whole.

There are yet other objects which have, or should have, throughout, strict reference to a specific end. Of this class are all buildings. These it may be thought may have beauty in themselves, — may please the eye, and, considered in reference to the end for which they were erected, have an additional beauty, and that the first may be conveniently termed absolute, and the second, relative beauty. But no building can be judged as a whole, as a building, without knowing the end for which it was built. This it was which called for the structure, — which gave law to the structure, which was everywhere in it as a plan and a purpose. It is a meaningless pile without the interpretation of this end, — this aim of labor, — and only becomes an expressive and beautiful thing as this object of rational effort, and the fulness and felicity with which it has been reached, are seen. It is not the eye, but the mind, that judges the work, and its inquiries at once are, What the object? and, How reached?

If the building has no beauty in its relation to an end, it has no beauty as a building. There may still be certain parts which can be considered separately, and pronounced beautiful, but the dwelling, the church, and the cathedral are what they are only in view of the end they subserve and the feeling that gives rise to them.

We cannot, therefore, here have an absolute which is not a relative beauty. The question of beauty is one, — Is the building as a building beautiful? — and for the right answering of this, all the relations and objects of the building must be understood.

LECTURE V.

THIRD CONDITION OF BEAUTY, TRUTH.—IMITATIONS.—TRUTH DEFINED. — CONNECTIONS OF NATURE AND ART. — THE IDEAL.

A THIRD characteristic of beauty is truth. This assertion, however, is only applicable to art, since nature is our standard of truth, and all natural beauty necessarily possesses this quality. So various and vague are the notions attached to the phrase Truth in art, that we shall not be able to make satisfactory progress without carefully defining its several meanings.

Some reference of art to nature, — some agreement of our conceptions with facts, — is supposed to be included in the words, though the precise connection intended, of man's creations with those of the external world is not seen.

A common meaning of the true is that by which it is confounded with the best, the noblest, the right. In this sense, to say that truth is a characteristic of beauty, may be either to utter the truism, that that which is best or beautiful is best or beautiful; or if, proceeding more wittingly, we first define what is the best, the noblest, the true, and afterward call this beautiful, it may be to perform the work already undertaken by us in showing what that is in expression which is beautiful. Of the true, then, as employed to designate that which is correct or high-toned in expression, we have no further occasion to speak.

A second meaning of truth is, that which excludes falsehood from art, and suffers no surface work to indicate, either in structure or material, that which does not exist beneath it. In this signification, the true is the genuine, and is especially at war with veneerings, paints, stuccos, frescoes, and cast ornaments; at least, so far as they purport to be other than what they are. An encouragement of these makes deception an end of art, and naked imitation its means, thus destroying the artist; gives rise to pretence, ostentation, and an ungrounded self-satisfaction in the employer of art, thus degrading him from the patron of virtuous taste to the pander of a false and foolish vanity; and reduces the enjoyment of art to the detection of a clever resemblance, leaving the critic now pleased with his own acuteness, now chagrined by his failure to discover the imposture.

It should certainly be an important principle with the lover of art to prefer the genuine to the false, a plain and substantial reality to elaborate and unsubstantial ornament; but so far have these surface dressings now entered into art as to render their exclusion both undesirable and impossible. Architecture is alone affected by them; and as this is primarily a useful art, ruled by economic principles, and only secondarily a fine art, it can never be made entirely amenable to the laws of the latter. It is evident, however, that all finish which is intended to suggest what does not really exist should be carefully excluded from high and valuable art, from public and monumental architecture. Let us, at least, know that that which claims to be good is honest; that that which arrogates merit is not a bold lie, challenging detection; that the people have not combined to do both a weak and a false thing.

In domestic architecture, on the other hand, which is expected to be more temporary, claims less for itself, and must be more economic, veneers and imitations will always play an important part, and this, too, without detriment to the taste of a people, if one or two things are remembered. The radical difficulty with this method of workmanship is the deception aimed at. It is this which gives rise to pretence and ostentation on one side, and disappointment and contempt on the other. Our true success, then, in this kind of art is not, as is supposed, in a completeness of imitation which misleads the mind, — and fortunately the supposed perfection is unattainable by most workmen, — but in an agreeableness of design and success of execution which, while pleasing, yet reveal themselves for what they truly are. Paint has not the best effect when it is thought to be good stone or the native wood, but when it is seen to be paint well put on. It then does an honest, valuable, and praiseworthy work. While the veining of wood may suggest a pattern, that graining is best which gives rise to no doubt, but in itself and in its relations at once shows that it is graining.

An agreeable impression may undoubtedly be secured by a cheap yet permanent surface work, and it would certainly be foolish to throw away papers and paints, which relieve and cheer the eye in every dwelling, because what is represented by them is often not real; nor is it difficult to draw important practical distinctions between the right and wrong methods of using these materials.

(*a.*) That which reveals its own nature is to be preferred to that whose success is dependent on a suggestion of something better than itself. Imitation should be turned aside from entire resemblance, and those features which mark the nature of the material be suffered, nay, made to appear freely. Iron-work will ever show itself to be iron, unless most assiduously disguised. A casting will naturally distinguish itself from a carving, and this it should ever be suffered to do.

The parts of the design must always be heavier and better sustained in stone, than when wrought in the tenacious fibres of iron. The inherent strength of the one material tends to a lightness of pattern quite impossible with the other. The more markedly every material possesses and wears its own characteristics, the better is it, and there is no so sure way of destroying both the higher and the lower, as a constant effort on the part of the one to assume the forms and draw to itself the attention which can only properly belong to the other.

(*b.*) That which is genuine should not be mingled with that which is imitative. This is often done on purpose to aid the deception, and must always have the effect to confuse the mind, and render it suspicious. Such a method is opposed to the frank, open spirit already urged, which everywhere avows its material by its manner of treatment.

(*c.*) That which is inaccessible and beyond our judgment should be in kind like that near at hand. No impression is more unfortunate than that our action will turn into an indolent subterfuge the moment it is out from under inspection. It is better to make the deception elaborate, place it where it may be examined, and defy detection, than to hide a cheap and lazy imitation in the distance, and then affirm it to be genuine by a witness near at hand. The spectator, when discovering the character of such work, feels that he has not been cheated by the cunning of the artist, but by his sheer, shirking dishonesty.

If these principles are regarded, an inability successfully to carry imitation into deception, and custom telling us what to expect, and in what places, will do the rest, and the various methods of surface treatment will be as genuine as any work in wood or stone, for they will only indicate what they really are. They may, also, well be the more dear to us, because they give early play to the fancy, and, accessible to all, are the modest adornments of the homes of the many. That truth which acknowledges its material, which honors the genuine, which marks the imitative as such, is an element of all correct taste.

This meaning of truth is, however, subordinate to yet another meaning employed in questions of art, the one more immediately referred to in speaking of it as a characteristic of beauty. This is an agreement between the signs and symbols of art and those of nature. The language of the two must be the same. What we have seen in the actual world must interpret what we see in the ideal world, and what is here present must have the fulness and force of what we have elsewhere felt. It is this common speech of art and nature, — this use of the same forms and colors, the same traces of life and indices of feeling, — that makes them one in their hold on the mind, and renders it impossible to enter into the first, save through the gateway of the second.

The plans in nature, while elaborate and varied, are sternly self-consistent, are, within the limits she herself has defined, forever the same. Each kind of tree has its own method of branching, each trunk its own bark-surface, each rock its own fracture, each moss its own pattern. Truth in all representation lies in the knowledge of these; and in representing them, — we are not limited to a fact, but to facts, not to a form, but to a method: and he who knows, neither by observation nor inspiration, how nature works, cannot himself work. No origination of symbols is open to the artist: he speaks as God has spoken from the beginning. There is but one alphabet of beauty, and that is found in nature. The relation of art to nature we must unfold more fully.

The first condition of beauty was given as expression. This is fundamental, it is that which underlies beauty, and comes out in it. The second was stated to be unity in variety, or, more simply, unity. This is not something in addition to expression, but the method of that expression, that without which expression itself is not beautiful. The third is now given as truth. This again is subordinate to, and modifies, the expression; unity was its method, truth is its means. It is utterance through natural and real, not through artificial and arbitrary signs. The expression stands in most immediate connection with things and facts, and thus is true. Beautiful expression in art is the unity of true signs in the utterance of worthy emotion. Nature in her work gives us the method, and our adherence must be faithful, — gives us the language of all dead and living forces, and our use of this must be, to the last degree, accurate.

Two things may seem to contradict this assertion, — the conventional and grotesque in art, and the arbitrary signs exclusively employed in poetry.

The conventional is that which by tacit agreement stands for something which it is not in itself able to represent. It especially appears in the carvings of architecture, where the completed form of the plant or animal escaping the chisel, a few strongly wrought lines take the place of finished work. The conventional, — and the same is true of the grotesque, — if wholly arbitrary, is not of itself beautiful, and becomes a mere member, like a moulding, to be judged solely by its relations, — by the general effect. It has no agreement, more or less, with nature, and hence there is no opportunity for truth. If, however, it boldly strikes at the reality, it may then become a curt truth, worthy in itself of consideration, though unable to tell all that might have been told. Intrinsic beauty here, however, as elsewhere, is dependent on the faithfulness of what is done, be it more or less.

In poetry, the signs are, indeed, wholly arbitrary; but the beauty is not in these, or what they present to the eye, but in the images presented through them to the mind, and these images must be faithful.

Rhythm, and a certain agreement of sounds with the thought, may enhance the effect to the ear, but only because there now begins to spring up a resemblance to the real, — a somewhat obscure truth. So far as poetry is representative, the necessity of truth is as great here as elsewhere. The possible, the probable, are counterparts of the real, and reached through it; and these assign limits to all poetic presentation, be it epic or dramatic, lyric or descriptive. Things that are, are facts; things that may be, are truths. Both contain the same principles, the same laws of being and action, the same appeal to the thoughtful mind, — the one, because it is; the other, through its agreement with that which is, because it utters the same lessons and the same laws.

The one contains beyond the other only the single item of a precise, historic existence. The actual, in its accidents, in its names and dates, has appeared but once; in its essentials, it is constantly reappearing, repeating itself at intervals everywhere through the complex pattern woven in the same loom under similar conditions. This it is which gives to the real its value, converting facts into principles and history into philosophy. This also is the truth of poetry. In emotion it utters that which may be, that, therefore, which a thousand times has been, and, in this its mastery of the actual, rules the heart. There is more truth in that which may often be, than in that which is known to have been but once. There is little value in any conception which has not that agreement with facts which makes it possible, probable, truthful.

Architecture is, in many particulars, not a representative art, and is, therefore, having no counterpart or standard in nature, to be judged by its own effect. The same is true, in a yet higher degree, of music. Truth, then, as a characteristic of beauty, must not only be limited to the fine arts, but yet further limited to those which have a correspondence or resemblance to nature, — that is, primarily, to poetry, painting, and sculpture.

It is in connection with these arts, and the quality of truth belonging to them, that we can best apprehend the relation of the real to the ideal, — of nature to art. The field which nature occupies she occupies not to the exclusion of man, but for his instruction and guidance. Though much in the world of living forms is not complete, the suggestion of completeness is everywhere present. The mind is not suffered to feel that it perfects a plan which the Architect of the world was not able to perfect, — that it discovers the failing strength of an art grand indeed in its rudiments, but unfinished, — and is called in to complete the too great undertaking. The execution is not pushed to a point at which the conception fails, but the outlines and plans are ever in advance of the work; and man, as a journeyman artist, is employed in the study and realization of these. Human genius, however powerful its command of beautiful forms, adds no new species either to the animal or the vegetable kingdom, — no new phases either to land, water, or cloud scenery. Its strength is fully tasked in the study and mastery of that boundless variety already present. The expression in nature is so manifold and powerful as more than to occupy the mind in its acquisition, — as more than to meet its utmost demand in bodying forth its own emotions; and man has thus neither ability nor occasion to add to the resources of æsthetical feeling laid open to him in the world of physical forces. The office of art is, here, not the invention in elements of that which is new, but the fresh and powerful use of that which is old, — of that which is familiar, of that whose power passes under the hourly observation of men.

Nature is the source of beauty, and our guide in its pursuit, since she gives us, in all their variety, the forms under which inorganic and organic forces in the progress of a creative plan present themselves The first steps in representative art are a full possession of all th› facts in the department considered, of what in nature is there uttered, and of the method in which it is uttered. It is no more possible to be eloquent to the heart through the eye without a careful realization of color and form, than to reach it through the ear without the vocables of familiar speech. Art must be strictly and protractedly imitative, till it has mastered the symbols through which it works; and that art will be most powerful which has best learned this its first lesson; that has put itself in complete possession of the only means through which it can afterward express its own feelings. These means of expression, which are form and color as existing in nature, we have spoken of as the signs, letters, symbols, rudiments, elements of art, in order that we might by these words mark the extent of the analysis which should take place in the study of the external world.

He who copies a single scene is strictly and solely imitative, adds nothing to what he has received, and is measured by it. The accurate sketch of a landscape, the painting of a portrait, imply skill, but no more creative power than the rehearsal of an oration. A step beyond this is to discern the beauty of single features in the objects presented, and, retaining these, to reproduce them in new combinations. Here the same sort of taste is employed in selecting and rearranging the material as in using the thoughts of others. It is not, however, till the mind has gone further, and seen in each form the law and method of the force which gave rise to it, — has seized its characteristics, and is able to reproduce it in a member or in a whole with something of the freedom and boldness of nature, who scorns to imitate or repeat herself, — that it has power over the means with which it may itself work. Such an art may paint landscape, without painting a landscape, — man, and not a man. It has the breadth of the species, and not the limitations of the individual, and while impersonating its own ideas, does so with the double range before its eye of the actual and the possible, of the seen and the suggested. This is to analyze expression into its elements, and, by the mastery of these, to hold the key of all combinations, both old and new. This is at once to rethink the thought of the writer, to bring to it the resources of a full vocabulary, and thus to make it forever one's own in possession and in use. It is an agreement of art with nature, in elements, in the changing types of form and color, full and various as these are, that constitutes truth, and makes it infinitely more than imitation. Truth is only fully present, when that power is possessed to which imitation is a means, and when, therefore, imitation is ready to be laid aside. To copy a rock, plant, or animal is one thing; to distinguish between its specific and individual characteristics, and to retain the one while ever varying the other, is a much higher thing. An art that does this is truthful: its productions fall into the classes of science, and belong to the cabinet, and not to the museum.

The first gift, then, of nature to art is the symbols of expression employed in works of beauty, through whose study and imitation they are acquired.

The second is the beauty conferred in external objects. The Divine thought, the Divine idea, is contained in these; and as the perfection of the end and of the means is discerned, as the conception is seen working itself out in successful and spontaneous completion, the mind is awakened to beauty, and receives her most choice and safe instructions. In the same school in which the elements of expression are acquired, the inventive power is so quickened and trained as to possess that which it may utter. It is in the studio of nature, in the presence of forces ever expending themselves, ever renewing themselves in beautiful forms, that art catches its inspiration, and finds its own energies of feeling fostered into creative power.

The third gift of nature arises partly from what may be termed the defect of her execution, and still more from the variety and fulness of beauty which she shows possible in all departments. Beauty in the external world is unprotected from accident, is left open, especially in man, to the trespass of the stern laws of retribution and the dire necessities of sin. It thus suggests much to the mind which itself does not reach, and gives to man an ideal in advance of the fact. Toward this ideal, man labors in joyful though hopeless pursuit, since each attainment does but enable him to enlarge, to perfect in conception the thing to be attained. This ideal is an angelic guide, with whom man travels an endless road between two antipodes, the imperfect and the perfect, the human and the divine. With only the real, man were stationary, but finding everywhere the suggestion of a better ideal, pursuing this, he becomes progressive.

The variety of expression open to effort concurs to the same effect. Beautiful objects are not all graduated to one scale. There is no optimism, excellency is shared among compeers. Beauty is not a balanced abridgment of universal virtue, but is the lustre of single virtues. While the mind delights in this or that expression, it does not thereby exclude from its pleasures even the counter expression. It presents as many shifting phases of feeling as the sky diverse forms of clouds. The variety in nature, while gratifying the mind, does not exhaust its power, and there still remain emotions which it would utter in its own way. The unceasing changes about it only teach it the power and scope of its materials, and these it makes haste to use in a kindred freedom of spirit. Nature, then, both in her defect and variety, teaches the mind to love and utter its own ideals, — ideals which perpetually enlarge before it, as it sees more of the force and vigorous methods of the beauty working in nature, more of the Divine idea of facts, more of the goal prophetically present in man, — ideals without which there would be possible no independent or valuable workmanship to man, no momentum of progress carrying him by a hair's breadth beyond the actual. The ideal is but the impulse received in our movements through the real, expended in the world of thought, and there wrought into that higher conception for which alone training and discipline are given. Without this momentum of the mind which reveals itself in new ideas, all scholarship would be acquisition, all knowledge, memory, all progress, patient trudging along the one thoroughfare of thought.

There are present in nature, —

(*a.*) Ideas, creating and arranging thought, — a feeling working itself out in happy and benevolent execution; and

(*b.*) Facts, things, often deficient, always varied, — now beautiful, now looking to a higher beauty somewhere and in some way to be realized.

There are in man, —

(*a.*) An appreciation of the facts in nature, — of the execution there present;

(*b.*) Of the suggestion in nature of the impulse which

it but partially obeys, partially completes. There is thus an ideal, an idea, a forming thought, furnished to man, and, at the same time, in the mastery of real symbols, a means, a material, on which this thought may work, in which it may realize itself.

Truth is the agreement of these symbols, these methods, with those of nature; and by it the works of man, no longer fantastic, are made akin to those of God, are truths in that they repeat the same great laws, and are but phases of the forces which work the world. The ideal of man working itself out truthfully becomes, as it were, a new and most significant fact amid the facts of nature, — working itself out nobly, becomes a new and redeeming fact amid the facts of nature. The artist taught by nature works with nature, rescues her from contravening and hostile forces, adds to her variety, and, seizing her best thoughts, labors on them in statue and painting.

Landscape gardening, an art presentative rather than representative, will furnish us a closing illustration of nature's treatment of man. By a skilful use of plants, shrubs, and trees, almost any spot can be greatly ornamented. The valley, grove, and brook-side, though beautiful, are not as beautiful as they may readily be made to be; and man is encouraged to effort both by the means furnished and the necessity imposed. There is sufficient beauty present in the untrained growth to call out his taste, and awaken his desires; and in the same instant a labor is imposed upon him, if he would employ and perfect the material ready to his hand.

Nor is this all: nature refuses her own wild beauty to one who fails to train and culture it. Every place becomes better or worse under the hand of man. All noxious weeds — slovenly and ragged in habit, offensive in odor, rank in growth, prolific in generation, with burred seed-vessel catching to man and beast — gather about and hunt down the sluggard, — avengers of nature's wrong. These make an admonition of every neglected home, and, nodding in unseemly, unprofitable growth about the cheerless dwelling, seem to say, "Out of thine own mouth I condemn thee, and complete thine own work."

There is no spot so void of beauty, so utterly deformed, as the unkept abode of man. It forfeits the rugged yet chaste beauty of nature, and is smothered with the teeming ugliness which its own filth engenders.

LECTURE VI.

SYMBOLS OF EXPRESSION. — FORM. — COLOR. — LIGHT AND SHADE. — MOTION. — SOUND.

Beauty, as a primary, underived quality, is incapable of a definition, and we have contented ourselves, therefore, with pointing out some of the conditions of its presence, — that in objects which is its occasion. The first given was expression, — a thought and feeling, an idea. But, as the expression itself is not the beauty, neither does all expression give rise to beauty, we endeavored to show further what, in plan and idea, have this additional power over the mind, quickening it to a new and most pleasurable perception.

The second condition given was unity, — a quality of expression by which it becomes a complete, in all its parts a concurrent, sentiment. The last condition stated, and one more restricted than either of the others, was truth. Nature has a method in which her ideas are uttered, under which her orderly forms act. Truth in art is an accurate concurrence of method with that found in corresponding facts. True art can always find both corresponding facts and corresponding methods, — corresponding facts, because its ideal has arisen under the suggestion and in the pathway of nature; corresponding methods, because it has been taught all its symbols by nature.

What these symbols are, what the things which to

the senses betoken and convey the idea, we shall now inquire. It is evident, that all these symbols of thought, and signs of feeling, must be such as present themselves to the senses, since beauty inheres in objects and actions, and these become subjects of contemplation through the senses, or the imagination, acting under the law of the senses. It is also evident that our several senses will be avenues to these signs only as they are capable of a clear presentation of the complex and the combined. The eye has, in this respect, the greatest power, and therefore becomes the chief medium of beautiful impressions. The ear, through language, gives to the inner eye of imagination the reflection and counterpart of external vision, and thus indirectly becomes a dependent, secondary avenue to beauty. In music, the sense of hearing opens a direct inlet to a distinct and full department of expression. The other senses drop abruptly below these two, are so single and local in the sensations which they confer, so lose their burden in the organ, and transfer so little to the intellect, and are so overborne and displaced by the higher organs, as not to be the instruments of taste.

The eye, the great highway of the mind, takes cognizance in extreme analysis of several distinct things.

Form is here the first great means of expression, — the most immediate and inevitable product of all arranging thought. Form is here used in its fullest signification, and includes not merely outlines, but superficies in all their tracings and irregularities. Expression, in opaque bodies at least, is limited to surfaces, to the arrangement of parts on these, and of these in reference to each other. Beauty, as veining, does indeed penetrate some bodies, but it only become manifest beauty by their section or cleavage.

Matter being given, the very first action of force is indicated by a change of form, and the nature of the resulting form is our only index of the character of the force, and of the thought which set the force in motion. Entire irregularity is confusion, is chaos, and a change from irregularity to irregularity is aimless and barren. An apprehensible form is the first product of creating power, which, the elements of matter all present, is nothing but arranging power. The more simple and mathematical the form, — for mathematics, in all its pride, reaches but first principles in the figures and curves which it discusses, and in the powers of nature whose action these restrict, — the more limited and rudimental is the force, and the more simple the idea indicated. The crystal and the sphere, which may be said to be the fulness of geometry, are reached in an instant, and everywhere are primal forms in nature's action. So restricted in expression are all regular figures, that but two arts employ them to any considerable extent, landscape gardening and architecture; the first, in any high state, always escaping into that which is freer and fuller; the second, though sternly circumscribed by its material and uses, yet, for its tracery and ornament, ever reaching up into the higher realms of animate nature.

As form feels, betrays, and measures every movement, every advance, of the creative thought, it must instantly become more complex as this gathers scope and power, — as the plan begins to include more, and the parts, standing in broader and more numerous relations, to suffer more modifications. Complexity of form will be measured by complexity of uses, — the number of offices performed by the instrument, the number of changes wrought in or with the machine. The instrument is more graceful than the machine, as more compact and single. God's work in nature is instrumental rather than mechanical. The body is rather the mind's instrument than the mind's machine; the plant, the agent of a living principle, than a manufactory of vegetable acids.

These two thoughts borne in mind, — that, with each advance of plan through the range of life, vegetable, animal, and rational, there is ever a more complex end, wider relations, and also a more immediate, instrumental, and personal use, by each living principle, of its own forces and organs, — and we shall at once see that form, in happy obedience to these new and numerous necessities, will have a wonderful revelation to make, both of the variety and ductility of material, and of the thousand chemical and mechanical processes which take place in and through it, without the heat of furnace or sound of wheel. Here is an opportunity in form for "the felicitous fulfilment of living function," — for a thought of love most skilfully executed, — for beauty. Form — pliant, flexible, full of office — becomes more and more the seat of thought, more and more able to mark the progress of the Creator's work.

As form is condensed and intensified in expression, — as every line and curve become significant, till within the breadth of the human face the character of all generations is written, — it will be observed that variety, though not less, is less bold, is held within narrower limits. If the machine combines but a few wheels, the position of any one may be readily changed; if many, this is done with more difficulty, for a system of complex interdependence is thereby broken. Plants of the same species differ widely from each other in the number, arrangement, and outline of their members. As the plan is not yet full or complex, it takes to itself more license, the relation of parts is more readily shifted, and by this change the freshness of expression is preserved, small differences are less obvious, and variety is secured with a bolder hand. The changes which make one tree to differ from another are as much greater than those between man and man as the plant is less expressive, less complete in its form, less complex in its organization and relations, than the man. The very amount and perfection of the work in the human body straitens the variety of form which it may assume, and yet adds to the power of the slightest change. While plants differ more from each other, they are less readily discriminated from each other than men. The human face, while true to itself in all leading characteristics, is, in the power of its variety, in the spiritual tidings which are signalled in it, unmeasured.

Akin to this is the number of species by which the beauty of the lower kingdoms is sustained, as against the higher. Contrast grasses with forest-trees; insects with birds and mammals. In preserving the balance, quantity is made, in part, to take the place of quality, and in the prodigality of workmanship, we lose the sense of inferiority. Man, while gathering into himself the crowning excellences of form, stands over against and outweighs a physical world, striking in every single feature, and marvellous in its range.

It has been questioned whether beauty has any real existence aside from the percipient. It has as permanent and independent an existence as that in which it inheres. Each advance of order upon disorder, of creation upon chaos, marks the presence of a formative idea, and this, as seen in its product, gives rise to the impression of beauty, not by virtue of anything in the percipient beyond a receptive power, but through a quality which, the object unchanged, remains in it the same for all rational beings. Beauty does exist as a permanent attribute of the appropriate expression. The progress of creation develops not simply truth, but beauty for all intelligences. Beauty is the form and aptness of appropriate truth.

As form, though greatly varied, though complicated and elaborate in details as presented in nature, is yet wholly subject to law, exists in every modification through reason and for a reason, is ever expressive of some new change of the living principle, some new uses and necessities, it is evident that this most fundamental symbol must be thoroughly studied, and only as it is accurately presented can any work claim to be in sympathy with an actual creation, representative of real forces, of that ever-present, efficient, and Divine idea which makes the world beautiful.

Ignorance may disguise discrepancies, but art must know what forms have been wrought out by what forces, what parts give perfect play to what powers. Such a knowledge of form is attendant upon a knowledge of the characteristic differences and necessities of each kind of life. One, through naked imitation, may, to a limited degree, learn the lessons of form; but so perfectly is form the result of a thought working in a given material toward a given end, that, sometimes at least, the artist may seem to seize the nature of the principle with which he deals, and, working in the very current of the stream, to shape the shores of the living powers as they run parallel with, or give way before, the ruling force.

The second symbol of beauty to the eye is color. This symbol seems to have a less intimate connection with the power at work, and therefore to be a less important medium of expression and of beauty than form. To our present apprehensions, color presents itself more as a matter of accident, more as a surface ornament, than as an inevitable product of the idea present, — as a part of that idea. This judgment of color is evidently partly, and may be completely wrong. As the mere accident which we deem it, color is still included within, is still a constituent of the design, for this admits of no strict, no real accidents. It has less, perchance, but, as a thing contemplated, its own share, of expression. If we recollect, also, that color is the result of the action of surface particles on light, it may be that the arrangement of atoms which secures one color rather than another, stands in more intimate connection than we now think with the very nature of the formative principle present.

As we have but a limited notion of the connection of color with the forces at work, and as, therefore, its speech — its expression — is in this direction restricted, we must look elsewhere for much of its power.

(*a.*) Most important among the considerations which indirectly impart power to color, is, that through it alone can complex form be brought out. Outline is independent of color, but the pattern of surfaces is greatly dependent upon it. We are readily deceived and led to ascribe to color what properly belongs to form. The veining of marble or of the petals of flowers, the variegated landscape, are beautiful, but largely through the pleasing forms presented and brought to the eye by different colors. Let the patterns be preserved, and, though the shades are changed, we may often find that the staple of our satisfaction remains. Wall-paper and other prints are so varied frequently, with only slight gains or losses. Not that the color is a matter of indifference, but that often when most important, this importance arises from its relation to the form, from the greater or less relief which it gives to it. Much, then, of the pleasure which we carelessly refer to color, is really to be referred to form.

(*b*.) The impressions on the organs of sense which different colors make are different.

Brilliant colors attract and please the eye, partly through novelty, partly through a stronger organic effect. Other more neutral colors rest the eye, and others, through their more common, obscure, and mingled character, producing no distinct effect upon it, suffer neglect. Colors, having these their sensuous impressions, when employed in connection with beautiful forms, are, according to their several natures, unpleasant, animating, or tranquil, and lend these characteristics to the object.

(*c*.) Colors come to the mind with various associations; that is, with an acquired power of expression. Brillant colors acquire gayety, and sombre colors yet more of sadness, from the scenes in which they figure. Imperial purple, funereal black, priestly white, and Quaker drab, have each their power greatly enhanced by the service to which they have been set apart. The plumage of a splendid bird or the tints of a fine flower may increase our partiality for particular colors. Azure, violet, and lilac, orange, olive, and rose, testify to the sources of different shades, and to their impression enhanced through association.

To a certain degree, inferiority is attached to color as a symbol, by the use which is made of it in the external world. Form is much more unchanging than color. Indeed, when the last is not fixed through a scientific necessity, as it were, that it may aid us in discriminating species, it seems wholly wayward. The rose, the tulip, the verbena, the China aster, have no limit to their wardrobe of shifting colors. A more significant fact, however, is that, while form becomes more complex and perfect from lowest to highest, no such gradation is found in color. The inorganic world presents some of our most brilliant displays in this respect; witness the gems and the clouds. The lower organic creations are, as a class, more showy than the higher; witness sea-mosses, shells, and insects. In man, color almost wholly drops away, or, if present, is so to limit, rather than to enlarge, expression. Solomon in all his glory was not arrayed like the lily. The distinction lay in color, not in form. Both the word arrayed and the fact are derogatory to color. Brilliant hues are added to the inferior by way of compensation; the superior is lifted above ornament, above array. The Caucasian blush, which is certainly the most significant use of color in man, derives its power not half so much from its character as color, as from the intimate and most unusual connection it is seen to have with the forces of life beneath. The power of the blush, beyond the pigment, beyond mere paint, is that it is seen to come and go. By virtue of this, it stands in the same intimate connection with the vital power as form. If all color were seen to be the suffusion of a vigorous or a virtuous life, it would instantly gain over us an entirely new power.

In this connection, it is worthy of remark, that while hair seems to man primarily an ornament, its chosen colors are shades of black, passing with age into white, — the only two negatives, — and that all brilliant color is alike uncommon and ungrateful.

The use of the terms gaudy and modest has also something of this disparagement of color. The perpetual variety which fashion feels called on to furnish is equally an abuse of form and color, and shows her action a fantastic pursuit of novelty, with but slight reference to taste.

While form is the basis and framework of beauty in the world, the most sensible and immediate part of the effect is often due to color. Much is appreciated through it which would otherwise remain unfelt. It lays hold more strongly of the senses, and, arresting us, leads us to a more intimate knowledge of form, and the more intellectual lessons there taught. The brilliancy, vivacity, and cheerfulness of the world are due to color; its depth of emotional power to form.

As there is a broad, careful, powerful, determinate, and appreciative use of color in the world, it, as a symbol of expression, claims most accurate study.

A third of those symbols which address themselves to the eye, is light and shade, — *chiaro-oscuro*.

This is certainly not less important than color. The one arises from light as a compound, the other from it as a simple. Color results from the decomposition of light on the surfaces of bodies; light and shade, from the interception and reflection of light by bodies. The one has reference to those modifications of light which affect its kind, as in the painting; the other, to those which affect its degree, as in the engraving.

Shade stands in more intimate relation with form than does color. As shadow, it is the repetition of outline under those regular but multifold changes which the relation of the body to the light occasions; as varying in intensity, it owes its variety to the form of surfaces.

Light and shade demand most careful study and treatment, both for the beauty of their effects and the number of truths which are committed to them.

The heavy shadows which lie along the valleys and choke the ravines at early day, as if the now broken forces of night were skulking in mountain retreats, and eluding the shafts of light behind every barrier, — the thronging shadows of evening which, aware of their hour, rally from their defeat, and come creeping forth from all their hiding-places, till they have again locked arms in solid phalanx, — the spectral shadows of a summer's night, dark as the angles of a city whose mystery and concealment take refuge even from the mild moon, — the rippling lake, flashing like a shivered mirror, or hiding another world beneath its surface; — all testify to the fascinating power of light and shade, and the large share of expression which has been committed to them. But this is not all, — a large allotment of truth has fallen to their share.

(*a*.) Time is given us by light and shade. Each hour of the day has its own character; — evening, its deepening, lengthening shadows to mark the waning movements; bold noon, its soft, diminished, penetrable shades ; and morning, its deep, strong outline, exultant light playing about the unwarmed and unpenetrated recesses.

To the question, When? within the circuit of the day, light and shade make answer.

(*b*.) Position and distance are in part committed to these. Strength of light indicates the near, dimness of light the more remote objects, while shadows, like a system of parallel lines crossing the landscape, help to mark the position of every object. Allied to this in its effect, is the color of the atmosphere. The deeper blue of the distant mountain and the lighter shade of the intervening vales, not only give a new variety to the scene, but define its relations. The heavens are not azure for beauty alone.

(*c*.) Our knowledge of form is largely dependent on changes effected by it on light. The shadow as much explains the building or the character of any solid to the eye, as the solid determines the shadow. So much are shadows and things the counterparts and charts of each other in every changing phase of light, that we hardly know for what share of our information we are indebted to the one, and for what to the other. Certain it is, that the eye arrives at form mainly through light and shade. Through this medium alone do plane surfaces represent to us every variety of solids. This is accomplished through different intensities of light, equally when color is present as without it. Every surface, of whatever color, is affected by the power of the light resting upon it, and the principles of light and shade have, in kind, the same application in a painting as in an engraving. Not an inch of canvas can be treated without reference to the effect of unequal light.

The inexhaustible variety of colors in the sky is due to the effect of light on the same material at different distances and angles. Whatever we paint, the convolutions of a cloud or of a garment, the relation of parts is found and told in the shifting shades. So susceptible is this subtile material, light, that each circumstance traces itself in a change of effect, and every effect, therefore, reveals a circumstance. So accustomed is the mind to this instant information which light gives through its own modifications, that it utterly fails to distinguish between that which is seen and that which is inferred, and is surprised to find the larger share of its visual knowledge of the latter kind. Changeableness, a susceptibility of endless degrees, is a prime quality of light as a revealing power.

(*d.*) Another class of implicated truths dependent on light and shade, to which we can only make reference, arises from reflection, the mingling of reflected and transmitted light. A stream presents three objects or scenes, sinking downward one below the other: the surface of the water, the bottom on which it rests, and the reflection of the banks. These may sometimes all be seen from the same position, and sometimes one to the exclusion of the other, according to the light and the point of the beholder. If a strong light is reflected from the surface, this alone of the three will remain visible, but let the shadow of a cloud fall on the stream and it will then yield prominently the image of the bank if the water is deep, if shallow, the bottom prominently, and the surface and the reflection obscurely.

A ripple, by multiplying reflecting surfaces and shifting their angles, will proportionately lengthen and diffuse the light, and will repeat certain objects, distort some, and omit others in the image below. To the conditions before present in simple light and shade, there are now added, in treating water, its depth and color, its transmitted and reflected light, its variableness of surface and of the light falling upon it. Upon these will depend from what quarter each object rendered to the eye shall come, whether from the space above, from the bisecting plane of the surface, or from the space beneath, and how these objects shall in transmission be modified. Yet each result obeys its own law, and has its own truth to tell.

The fourth visible symbol of beauty is motion. This is expressive in several directions.

(*a.*) The rapid motion of great bodies in straight lines or in simple, prescribed curves, through the power implied, affects the mind with the feelings of sublimity. Indeed this species of beauty is largely dependent on motion present or implied, since through this we chiefly receive the impression of strength. The volume of momentum, and the amount of power therein obviously indicated, are the essential points. A large mass of clouds, by the ease and silence of a movement not apparently rapid, excites the mind. Momentum, which is the product of volume and velocity, must be great to impart sublimity.

The want of bulk may in part be compensated by rapidity, and the want of rapidity by bulk. Yet, as all small bodies affect feebly the mind, velocity, however great, cannot wholly atone for deficiency in mass. The bullet and the cannon-ball are not sublime. If our conception could keep pace with the fact, the motion of the heavenly bodies is, in this direction, the culmination of the sublime.

(*b.*) Motion in free, undefined curves may give the impression of beauty. Motion in straight lines and defined curves is mechanical, secured by a dead force; motion in free and undefined curves is animate, secured by a living force. The one — we speak not of what is always, but of what is usually true — indicates power received and obeyed, and becomes of interest only in masses; the other, power originated and self-directed, and has an independent life and value when lodged in the most limited compass. There the expression is of ease, pleasure, and grace, of the fulness of the vital force, and of its perfect self-control. The significancy of form is interpreted through motion. The chief adaptations of form are to motion, and the entire necessity and compactness and symmetry of the parts by which it is secured are not fully apparent till seen and explained in vigorous use. Attitude is but arrested motion, bringing out peculiar adaptations and energies, and making them the object of more prolonged attention. The full force of form is only seen in motion, and in pleasurable and powerful motion the beauty of animate objects passes to its height.

The two extremes of movement are represented by a ball driven under impact, and by man in the variety of motions which belong to his marvellously ductile organization. The one starts in simple force, the other ends in all the varied applications and uses of force which belong to the combined necessities of physical, intellectual and spiritual life. In the barren and simple rudiment, power, there is yet often present high sublimity.

(*c.*) Between these extremes there is an intermediate ground, where motion is neither wholly mechanical, nor wholly vital: such are the waving of the forest and, to the fancy, the running of the brook. The elastic rebound of the one and the easy indolence of the other chime in with moods of mind, and add distinct and changeable elements to the scene.

The first symbol to the ear is words. These, however, aside from rhythm, — a species of music, — are nothing in themselves, stand only as arbitrary representatives of other things, and are, therefore, in their subject-matter included in the other means of expression. The imagination works through words, the eye works without them, but both work upon the same objects.

Sound, on the other hand, as modified in music, becomes a distinct and most powerful symbol of expression, the only one given in any other sense than that of sight. Music, standing by itself in its own sense, is of all the fine arts most isolated and independent, of all the fine arts requires the most peculiar gifts and individual training.

Poetry, painting, sculpture, architecture, and landscape gardening, given in their symbols through the eye, are intimately connected, and the training of one prepares for that of the others. Not so with music. It is possible to be a musician, and to be nothing else; to be everything else, and not to be a musician.

Music probably acts more directly on the feelings than any other fine art. The intellectual element is weaker, the emotional element stronger; the immediate and powerful effect it has upon all classes indicates this. It is not the language of thought, but of passion; and in swell and dirge gives direct impulse to emotion. Music seems capable of employment, with slight modi fications, in most angelic and devilish service, as a quickener of holy love and lascivious lust. This is explicable on the ground of its strictly emotional character. The person addressed furnishes the emotion, pure or impure; music inflames it, and wafts it on, — the saint soars heavenward, the reveller sinks hellward.

The ordinary avenue, the well-trodden highway to the heart, is through the intellect. Music seems to have a path and gateway thither of its own. This is indicated by the facts, that no combination of intellectual powers gives any promise of musical perception; that this is an original gift which nature bestows, unquestioned, on her favorites; and that classes and races relatively uncultivated yet have a passionate love of music, and high powers of execution. No power is certainly less within the reach of mere cultivation than music.

The fulness and depth of this form of expression must render him, the postern gate of whose ear has been locked, an acknowledged unfortunate, though without the implication of any, the slightest, restriction either in the range of thought or feeling. If the doctrine entertained by some physiologists be true, that the cochlea is the musical instrument of the ear, whose special function it is to determine the gradations and consequent harmonies of sounds, it is plain that a physical defect or derangement at this point must interfere with perception, and of course, through this, with appreciation.

These are the symbols of a strictly intellectual quality, beauty; and, as coming all, with one exception, through sight, they witness to the pre-eminence of that sense.

It may be thought that in the symbols now given,

no adequate provision is made for moral beauty. The adjective beautiful should not be withheld from character, but it belongs to it rather as conceived in the concrete, than in the abstract, rather as seen in feature and action, than in any even balance and perfection of qualities given in barren statement to the intellect. Spiritual force, like every other, is revealed as beautiful in and through its own product, and this is visible.

LECTURE VII.

FACULTY THROUGH WHICH BEAUTY IS REACHED.—STANDARD OF TASTE.—WHY DISAGREEMENTS.—TASTE, HOW CULTIVATED,—THROUGH KNOWLEDGE, PURITY, IMAGINATION, AND FANCY.

HAVING discussed beauty as a quality, that in which it inheres, and the signs by which it presents itself, we reach in order the faculty,—the mental power, which arrives at this attribute. Here three suppositions are open to us. This quality is an external intuition, an object of one or all of the senses; or it is a deduction,—the result of reflection, and reached by reasoning; or it is an internal intuition,—the object of a superior rational sense.

The first is not tenable; for, if beauty were the direct object of any one of the senses, every one possessed of this sense would apprehend it directly and fully. Beauty would be as open to the perception of the brute as the man, of the uncultured as the cultured. The reverse of this is true, and no acuteness of senses is found to secure this perception.

The second is not tenable; for, as already shown, beauty is a simple and primary quality, and no such quality is the product of reasoning or judgment. No synthesis can reach that which is not combined, no analysis that which is not contained as a constituent in anything higher than itself. These two processes of reflection, therefore, have no power over beauty, and, if falsely applied to this idea, they immediately destroy it in its own peculiar nature, and confound it with some of the ideas of which they can take cognizance, as utility and fitness.

The third supposition, then, alone remains to us, that this notion is reached through an internal sense, an intuitive power of the reason. Nor is the necessity of the supposition its only proof. We have seen the quality, beauty, not to inhere directly in an external object, as sweetness in the peach or color in its rind, but indirectly through certain other ideas and relations there present, as right belongs to an action which has certain bearings on the welfare of men.

The basis of beauty, that in which it is discerned, may be said to be intellectual, and not sensual,—a conception, and not an object; form, and not matter; an idea, and not the material which that idea orders. While, then, there is an intuition, we see it cannot be an intuition of the senses, for these only furnish matter in its properties, only act on the material, and the present intuition, going beyond this, must find its quality in a conception, an idea, itself apprehended and present by means of a sensation. The intuitive action, therefore, which reaches beauty must be preceded by sensation, and be able to make the conception which sensation furnishes the mind its own object. In each material thing which is the product of design, there are present form and color, given in sensation, and the design, the plan which these indicate, given in the intellect. It is this intellection which becomes the object of the intuition.

In a cognition of beauty, the steps are three; two presentative and one perceptive: an object given in sensation; an action of the mind upon this object, by which it is understood, by which the idea in it is reached; the action of the reason on the idea, as unfolded in the intellect, and found in the object. The first and third of these steps are intuitions, the second, reflection. The third completes the others, and alone renders the quality beauty. The brute eye may perform the first, a simple power of thought, the second, and only a mind gifted with the high, intuitive organ, reason, the third. It is not strange that the preliminary steps, especially the second, should be confounded with the third; that the reasoning processes, by which objects are understood in their relations, should be thought to furnish a quality of which they are the necessary antecedents; that the presence of a new power, by which we reach in the old a fresh and underived attribute, should be overlooked.

The object in other intuitions of the reason is an intellection, and, in this respect, beauty is entirely analogous to truth and right. The proposition as presented to the eye is not seen to be a truth. It is only when the reasonings which pertain to it are perfected that the reason, acting on it as now presented, pronounces it a truth. This is yet plainer in the perception of right. The action merely is given through the eye; nothing is as yet declared about it. It may be the product of intelligence, and thus right or wrong, and it may be the result of idiocy or insanity, and thus be destitute of the higher attribute. The fact alone is before the mind, and not its circumstances, its sources, and results. On this fact, however, the mind proceeds to act, determines the motive, inquires into the immediate and ultimate results of such action, and the degree in which its author understood these, or could have understood them. The action, in all its relations being laid open, the reason then discerns in it as so presented the quality, right, or the disregard of that quality, wrong.

The correctness of the reference of beauty to an intuitive faculty will be more and more seen at every step. So radical is it, that all minor truths explain it, and are explained by it.

The inquiry now arises, whether the decisions of taste tend to a common result — whether diversity is accidental and agreement permanent. The answer to this question must depend on the intuitive faculty, on the further question whether this admits in its action variety or is the same for all. The reason must be the final referee in questions of beauty, equally in nature as in art, and if its judgments conform to no law, and establish no standard, then there is no basis of agreement or of science in this department. The individual may have his own principles; but as between individuals all is caprice. Nature and art in their variety may be judged, but as sustaining this or overthrowing that judgment nothing can be said.

That the intuitions of reason agree with themselves, and establish a standard, is sustained by arguments plain and familiar, and requiring but a brief presentation.

It is probable that an intuitive organ, whose office it is to impart, to perceive, would, in the same things, perceive and impart the same qualities.

If such an organ is a source of knowledge, renders truth, it must yield that which is objectively present in things, and this must be the same to every recipient. Our physical senses, it may be said, are not accurate, admit of considerable variety, and render a similar discrepancy probable at other points where it is less easily detected. Taste affords an illustration of this disagreement. To this it may be answered, that this variety is not such as to interfere with the office of this sense, that the organic impression is relatively much greater in the lower than in the higher organs of sense, that pleasure, rather than knowledge, is there aimed at, and that it is consistent, therefore, both with the nature and office of the organs of taste and smell, that these should, more than other organs, modify what they transmit. The eye and the ear, on the other hand, — the great gateways of knowledge, — we have every reason to believe, if we cannot always prove it, give the same information to all. The reason is the organ of our highest intuitions, is utterly destitute of any organic sensation or satisfaction, and is solely dependent for the enjoyment which it confers on the knowledge it transmits, on the quality whose presence it affirms. If, then, this quality has not a substantial existence, witnessed to by this faculty, the veracity of the faculty is impeached, its pleasure is an hallucination, and we have in our intellectual apparatus a power which avouches a truth where no opportunity for such a truth exists, and leaves us, not only satisfied, but delighted with the falsehood. This presents a case wholly different from any variety in pleasurable sensations. That an organ whose office it is merely to receive and to testify to its own impressions should show some discrepancies, is not strange; but that an organ whose office it is to report the most important and controlling principles in the realms of things, of belief, of action, which has committed to it beauty, truth, and right, should involve the mind in an inextricable labyrinth of falsehood, or, rather, through the want of any standard, destroy all idea of truth, is wholly inconceivable, utterly destructive of all faith in our faculties. A scepticism so radical destroys itself. Beauty is the most universal law of form, the most potent guide of method found in the external world. It includes all lower utilities and adaptations, and adds for the reason of man a most magnificent utility of its own. Beauty and utility are not dissevered or conflicting, but concurrent ends. Beauty includes the perfection of uses, and only in such manifest perfection is there beauty. If, then, this principle, which rules the external into a noble completeness, which is everywhere present, securing perfection and symmetry of plan, and skill of execution, is visionary, well may we afterward expect that the principle of right, giving form to moral action and truth, shaping all belief, should, being witnessed only by the same faculty, be also found illusory.

A second proof of the integrity of our intuitions is the practical faith which all men repose in the decisions of reason, and which they evince by reasoning with their fellows. This perpetual resort to argument implies, not only that there is common ground, common and truthful faculties acting upon facts, but a reasonable expectation that, with explanation and increased insight, corresponding views and convictions may be reached. Without a unity, a oneness of powers, all such methods were utterly useless and absurd. How, then, do we always deem them rational, and often find them successful?

A third consideration is the agreement actually existing among men on questions of taste. This may seem an inversion of the chief argument of our adversaries, — the disagreement among men concerning the things thought beautiful. Every belief, however, must, in the last appeal, rest, not on argument, but on a skilful and careful interpretation of facts. We shall shortly point out the occasion of variety in men's intuitions, and now note the kind of agreement in their judgments which, amid all discrepancies, indicates a radical unity of taste.

(*a.*) An agreement which becomes more complete as men better understand each other and themselves, indicates a oneness of controlling principles. A superficial agreement is most striking at the outset, and is rapidly lost as investigation proceeds. The reverse is true of a deep, interior unity. In all questions of taste, the lines of opinion, as they come up through the progressive stages of civilization, are found to converge.

(*b.*) Akin to the proof of unity, derived from the greater agreement of the masses as they pass up in intelligence, is the fact that in each community, while the violence of controversy is found with artists and connoisseurs, here also is found the greatest number of admitted principles. The controversy and the principles equally prove that the right, though disputed, is felt somewhere to exist.

(*c.*) A concurrence in the kind, though not in the degree, of awards which different persons assign the same work, evinces a unity of principles, with only a transient variety in their application.

(*d.*) Disagreements which are themselves perpetually changing, settling into no law, agreements which, once established, are becoming principles, more and more controlling, unite to show the accidental character of the former, and the inherent and radical nature of the latter. As, amid all discrepancies, there is yet in the facts these essential agreements, they obviously demand for their explanation a likeness of powers, and an ever increasing sameness of action.

It is not now a difficult task to assign a reason for the transient varieties of opinion everywhere so obtrusive. We saw the second step by which an intuition is reached to be the transformation of a sensation into a conception, an idea; in other words, the apprehension, on the part of the intellect, of the thought, the plan, contained in the object. Now, as the external and internal relations of the object are often most complex, and this thought, therefore, most deep and inclusive, it is not strange that the mind should reach it with difficulty and imperfectly; if with difficulty, its own task-labor and the slipping grasp of the understanding will weaken the impression of the object, and mar its beauty. Indeed, what is secured with the fatigue and delay of intellectual action is rarely regarded as beautiful; the mind demands the rapidity and fulness of vision. If the thought performs its work imperfectly, each imperfection will limit and modify the reason's estimate of what it has obtained, and an inevitable variety spring up in its decisions. This very variety marks how closely the reason clings to the truth of the fact before it, limiting its own judgments by the limitation which the intellect has already imposed on it. It is plain that the idea or conception which is furnished to the reason, and in which alone it sees beauty, will be as various as the powers and culture of the minds whose product it is, and that there must therefore be kindred discrepancies in the decisions of taste.

It is not affirmed that the reason sees the same beauty

in different conceptions, but in the same conception as realized in an object. But no complex object replete with thought communicates precisely the same impressions to understandings so various in their native and acquired powers as those of men. We find our most apt illustrations in the kindred questions of right.

Right inheres in action, but the reason cannot safely pronounce on action till it sees it; that is, till it knows it in its motive, its present relations and final consequences. But an exhaustive inquiry of this sort is often most laborious, and the intellect doing its work weakly, wickedly, or indolently, the reason is left to pronounce on a partial or perverted statement of facts, and hence to give a verdict, not only at war with truth, but with other verdicts given with kindred carelessness.

Here also we see the force which belongs to argument. It does not persuade or warp an intuition; this, the premises being given, is as fixed as fate. It strives to modify the premises, to affect the intellectual conception on which the reason is to pronounce. Either for right or for wrong, it leads the unbribed taste and conscience to its own position, as Balak, the incorrigible prophet, to Zophim, that it may have its enemies cursed from thence. Not more numerous on the retina of the eye than on the field of thought are the possible presentations of a given landscape; the very variety, therefore, which seemed at first to impeach the reason acquits it. This judge of things and actions, incorruptible in itself, has yet no power of investigation. Wicked witnesses and hired advocates may so render the facts as to make of no avail its integrity, and the united falsehoods of the heart and the head find transient currency under its seal.

The faculty, reason, is incapable of any direct culture. Like the eye, it seeks at once, and only seeks exercise. Taste, however, — for it is better to include in this term the presentative as well as the perceptive action of the mind, — may be trained, and that chiefly through the second of the steps by which a judgment of the reason is reached.

Of these three, the first is intuitive, the second reflective, and the third again intuitive; the first sensational, the second intellectual, the third rational; each part of our triple nature uniting in the judgments of taste. Action is the strengthening agent of our intuitive faculties; our reflective powers, on the other hand, are, in addition largely dependent for their present efficiency on past work, on facts disposed of and principles established.

The rapidity and correctness with which the mind arrives at judgments on new matter presented to it, depend almost wholly on the use which it has hitherto made of its reflective powers, gathering up and explaining the phenomena about it in appropriate principles. So far as it understands the forces and laws at work in a given department, and has familiarized itself with every class of facts, will it be able at once to refer each new appearance to its appropriate place, and give to a reflective process the quickness and ease of an intuition. In this direction is it that the mind is chiefly disciplined. If the field is that of æsthetics, all knowledge which acquaints the mind with the office and habits of any flower, shrub, tree, insect, bird, or beast, will enable it the more perfectly to comprehend its form and adaptations, and through these the plan which, in its perfect execution, renders it beautiful.

All knowledge which acquaints the intellect with the force of the several symbols of expression, and enables it readily through these to reach the formative thought, which defines the conditions under which alone the mind receives pleasure, and makes familiar the principles which rule our enjoyments, will prepare the way for speedy and just decisions of taste. He whose past experience is classified and labelled, does not start anew in each judgment, but has the labor of past years at instant command.

In morals, he who has long and cautiously applied the laws of action to the questions of life, will be able speedily to refer each new case to its appropriate explanatory principle, and, with an intuitive faculty no more just and certain in its action than that of another, reach his conclusion with all the correctness and wisdom which have characterized his past elementary judgments. Many of the considerations which guide in questions of taste, and which are ever present to the wise critic, are still to be pointed out, but enough has already been done to show that the reflective processes, which prepare the way for a speedy and safe intuition, are so numerous as to render skill the result of much training.

Most of the questions of life are so complex as to require many antecedent judgments for their resolution. These each man brings with him, and according as they contain the complicated errors or the corrected wisdom of a life, will be the immediate result. False figures once introduced into the solution of a problem, are carried on and multiplied through the whole process. The chief method, then, by which we reach correct intuitions is a careful formation of elementary and preliminary judgments.

A second method of culture is securing integrity and purity in our own spirits. Health is requisite to the love of that which is healthy; and a lascivious, lustful heart will seek lascivious and lustful art. If the wisdom and grace of the thought, as it comes out in a noble product, are alone to elicit our admiration, there must be an intense sympathy in the spirit with that which is grace-giving and true, and a stern rejection of that which is wayward and ready to slip into base debauchery. The great bulk of error in morals, we know, is traceable back of the intellect to the inclinations, whose servants the thoughts are. The mind has not done its work well, because it has not been left free to take its own positions, but has been made to fortify each outpost of vice in which the heart chose to tarry. In a less degree, yet in a very sensible and unfortunate degree, men have weakened their appreciation of true beauty, and especially of human beauty, through a want of sympathy with the noble and true impulses which inspire it.

The world is full of God's conceptions, and he who would enjoy them must at least have sympathy with God as a worker. If to be high and to be holy are the same in man, or at least the completion of the same impulse, then he will best understand the high who rightly apprehends the holy. We here and everywhere deny beauty to that which is seen to degrade; and it is certainly true that a spirit firm in its own integrity, and waiting ever for the Divine word, will only see beauty in that in which it sees truth and worth. Beauty, though the weaker of the three, is never totally disjoined from truth and right, never keeps company with entire falsehood and baseness.

So akin, also, is reason in its several kinds of action, so allied are the reasoning processes by which we prepare the way for its several intuitions, that all training in the search after right will aid in the discipline of taste. This connection is sufficiently shown by the constant reference we have had occasion to make, for purposes of illustration, to the department of morals. In both departments there are subtile laws of action, each with its own imperative, the one weaker, the other stronger. He who can neglect that which is right in action will readily neglect that which is beautiful, and he who can despise that which is beautiful in action will the more easily despise that which is right.

What has now been said of the culture of taste, while leaving in their validity the decisions of reason, yet shows the impossibility of an absolute and perfect standard for the present guidance of men. Indeed, no such thing is desirable if so applied as to preclude that progress which with man is infinitely more than immediate possession. No decision of taste, however correct, can be seen to be correct save by one who has equally thoroughly canvassed the conditions on which it rests. How many soever, therefore, there may be of right judgments on the beauties of nature and art, these judgments do not stand forth with any peculiar lustre as guides for men till the public taste has itself arrived at that point in which it can appreciate and confirm them.

No individual can much avail himself of a standard higher than his own. Under the training of more powerful minds, he bears his own standard on, and the height of his achievement is marked by the position at which he at length halts. The possibility of entire and universal correctness, and hence of uniformity in the decisions of taste, is the possibility of entire fulness and precision in our reflective processes, and perfect integrity in our impulses. Such a state is a remote ideal, approximated by slow and laborious, yet constant progress. The ideal is ever something to be won, and not given, to be possessed in trained and conscious power, and not in native capabilities. It is the possible waiting to be made real in effort, the latent to be revealed in action.

It remains, in connection with the faculties by which beauty is arrived at, to point out the action of the imagination, and the distinction between this and fancy. Imagination finds its most constant employment in reproducing that to the eye of the mind which has been given in the senses. The impressions of the senses are transient, but the mind does not lose its power over them; when they have passed from these, its external organs, it is yet able to recover them and repeat them to itself through the faculties of memory and imagination. The memory guides the imagining power, and this reconstructs on the mental field what was before contained in the organ of sense. This takes place most distinctly in the matter given in vision, and it is sufficient for our present purpose to confine our attention to this sense, through which chiefly the symbols of beauty enter.

Not only does the imagination render to us copies of scenes remembered, under the guidance of description, it constructs more or less accurate representations of things reported by others, and in vacant hours gives medleys, scraps of many things before present to it. Nor is this all; while never escaping from the form under which the senses work, it often, under the influence of desire, renders combinations and images which, as a whole or in appreciable parts, may never have been seen or described. The air-castles of every enthusiastic dreamer are of this character.

Desire gives the law and subject-matter of the picture, and imagination paints it. There is a perpetual tendency to furnish out these scenes from the storehouse of memory, and yet they are often far from being mere counterparts of remembered objects. The imagination is thus a facile instrument in the hands of desire, bringing immediately before the appetite a full gratification, and perpetually inflaming it with its tantalizing proffers. All the lures of effort are lodged in the imagination, and thus it becomes a potent means of good or evil in the mind's government.

This same power not only works under the impulse of passion, but under that of reason, and realizes for the mind its intuitions of beauty. When the mind has mastered the symbols of expression, and has in it a feeling to be uttered, the imagination, under the guidance of reason, unites the two, and a distinctly uttered sentiment, a realized beauty, a creation, lies before the mind. The impulse, the feeling, is furnished by the heart, the conception which beautifully utters it by the reason, the symbols of utterance by past observation, and the realization of these to the vision of the mind by the imagination.

The reason acting on that given in the senses is simply intuitive and critical; acting with the imagination, is creative and productive, and thus supplements nature with art. The imagination then comes in to aid and realize the highest mental efforts, and the mind, no longer merely recipient — cultured and watered — begins to blossom and bear fruit.

There is another action of the imagination, less high and valuable than this, which is appropriately termed fancy. It is a pleasing rather than expressive use of form and color, — that limited play which is given to this creative faculty in schools of design.

Members pleasant in themselves are united in agreeable lines, and without compassing any thought the plan returns gracefully into itself. There is not disorder, nor yet is there any significant order. There is not a completion and correspondence of members, nor is each absolutely fragmentary and unconnected. A half-aimless and half-idle, yet ever graceful and powerful, movement of mind is indicated, with here and there single strokes in fine perfection. This fantastic, sportive movement of a mind too unoccupied to feel deeply, and too full to do anything absolutely meaningless, is fancy.

It is evident that the lower and the higher action of imagination, art and fine art, cannot be cut asunder by a straight and well-defined line. Genius at work employs imagination, at sport, fancy. Each is the same reproductive faculty, under a higher and sterner, or lower and milder, impulse.

LECTURE VIII.

PRINCIPLES WHICH CONTROL THE PRESENCE OF BEAUTY.—SUBORDINATION OF BEAUTY.—INCIDENTAL CHARACTER.—CONGRUITY AND PROPRIETY.—NUDE ART.

HAVING spoken both of beauty as a quality, and of the faculty by which it is apprehended, we purpose now to present some of the principles which control its manifestation.

The first may be concisely termed, the subordination of beauty. By this is meant its constant submission, its perpetual subservience to the end proposed, and the material employed in any given work. Each wise undertaking has an object furnished by the higher or lower necessities of life, and beauty comes in, not to control or turn aside, but to shape and perfect the means by which this is reached. She does not work for herself, but finds her gains in another's service. The plant does not live for beauty, but in beauty. Its leaves and petals have all primary reference to its own necessities, and life being ultimate, the methods and instruments of that life are made beautiful. So it is in architecture. The building has an adequate object, if not, it were folly to rear it, and beauty is the scope and mastery of means. The subordination of beauty is the constant reference of that which is beautiful to an ulterior end.

This principle arises from the very nature of beauty

as already presented. It inheres in an expression, — in a thought; now this expression, this thought, must have a reference, a significance of its own. That which is shaped under thought, is shaped toward an end, and thus, that anything may be beautiful, it must first possess a design, a completion, that which may make it an object of the intellect.

Wholly aside, then, from its beauty, there is in it a law and order, and this additional, this superinduced quality is only present through a perfect reference of parts to a whole, and of the whole to an intelligible end. In order of thought, then, if not of time, a conception containing its own end, and a realization of this conception, are prior to beauty. It is in the adequacy, fitness, and fulness of the means gathered up in a single purpose, that the reason perceives beauty. The object, in the completeness of its relations, must be given, before there is any opportunity for the intuition of beauty.

Beauty is not, therefore, itself a direct end, but springs up perpetually in the path of benevolent thought as it pursues other ends. It is an additional reward of well-doing, — the flower and the fragrance of the fruit-bearing tree. Like the satisfaction of virtue, it is not the direct object of the act from which it springs, but its inevitable and most pleasing reward.

The world having been made for man, no explanation of the presence of any substance, of any plant or animal, is felt to be wholly satisfactory till its immediate or mediate ministration to some one of the wants and pleasures of man is pointed out. Man is regarded as the ulterior reference of all things, the final consumer of all products, — the possessor of all possessions, the focus of all use, the head and summit of all enjoyments. But the necessities of man lie in three directions; in physical use or utilities, in intellectual use or instruction, in spiritual use or training. All below him, therefore, if explicable in connection with him, must, in existence and action, have reference at least to one or other of these three ends. There is probably nothing which, if perfectly understood, would not be found to include them all. Our knowledge of the complicated dependences of vegetable and animal life constantly increases. The humblest plants first creating, and then enriching, the soil on which the rankest and most immediately valuable grow, — each blade and leaf the grazing field of its own insects, and each tribe of these fattened for the maw of a neighbor, life balanced against life in most intricate compensations, — the greedy hunting of one class weighed with the fecundity of another, and the obvious concentration of lower plants and animals in the uses of the higher, — render the assertion not extravagant, not even improbable, that each external object may have utility, a final reference to the physical well-being of man. Certain it is, that a little thought is able to point out ends of instruction or of training in every object which reaches the eye.

All that our present purpose, however, requires us to affirm, is that there is present in each form of matter some service to be performed, some thought to be communicated, or some impulse to be imparted, and that in its happy obedience to a noble use alone lies its beauty.

This secondary and contingent existence of beauty does not mark it as inferior, or as less a contemplated object in the Divine plan. Man's physical nature in many directions sets limits to his spiritual powers, and brings forward its own wants as primary, but does not thereby prove that the intellect was lodged in the body to be its skilful servant, its sagacious purveyor. God makes instruction throughout the world apparently subordinate to utility. Utilities are reached through wise means, and in a wise harmony of enjoyments, and it is by an inquiry into the interior functions and uses of things that we receive divine instruction. Our lesson is locked up in objects which were made to minister to our wants, and seems no broader than their and our necessities, — no broader than utility required it to be. Divine wisdom is put to the service of making a useful and comfortable world. But this does not prove that the knowledge imparted in such a world was less a consideration in the Divine mind than physical gratification. The pulp of the peach is the utility of the peach-tree, and in securing this its beauty and wisdom are involved. The agility and strength of the horse are its utility, and in the means by which these are reached lie the wisdom of its structure; but neither is wisdom nor beauty therein shown to be a less important gift than agreeable fruit and rapid travelling. Of the three objects of our rational intuitions, beauty, truth, and right, the last only is ever, by its own nature, an ultimate aim of action. We may, and should, pursue the right for its own sake; not thus either knowledge or beauty. Knowledge is power, and power is an instrument and not an end. An avarice of knowledge has in it the same sort of fallacy as the poorer avarice of gold. Truths are the beacons which light up the path of success and skill, which show how and where the ends of life may be reached, which guide the eye to the storehouses of nature, and teach us to arm ourselves for high and bold achievements. Truth, knowledge, is the road to good, but not that good itself, — is potency, and not virtue, capability, and not possession. It may stoop in its ministrations to a physical, or mount to a spiritual good, but its own true value is not discovered till it is harnessed to a service. Beauty, on the other hand, is neither an end nor a means, but springs from the perfection of the means which concur in and complete an end. This intuition rewards skilful art, — all that escapes the mechanical and compulsory, and shows itself, in the impulse which gave rise to it, spontaneous, creative, and thoughtful. It is the seal of perfection which gives her work precedence.

This conception of beauty implies its subordination. As a seal, there must be that to which it may be affixed. As arising from excellences, yet itself no one nor even the aggregate of these excellences, there must be an object independently excellent as the source of this quality. According, then, as this independent perfection is everywhere regarded will the additional attribute be also realized.

In the thing or action which is beautiful there may be present, as a primary object, either a material or moral end, a utility or a good, a want met or a sentiment uttered. The first of these may seem, of the two, inferior, and the beauty which is dependent on a physical use to be disparaged by contrast with that which springs from a presentation purely intellectual. Our judgment at this point may be modified, however, if we reflect that natural beauty is everywhere included within material and physical ends, and comes in, like the grace of household furniture, to give to commonest wants a form of cheerful elegance. When the manifest aim of any object is a utility, the principle of subordination requires that that aim shall everywhere be prominent and pre-eminent; that form is to be adopted which most obviously and perfectly subjects itself to, and facilitates the use required of it. The conditions, the fixed points, are given by the end in view; and freedom and ease of transition are reached with these as a framework and basis, and cannot demand the exclusion or partial repression of any one of them. This is the problem: Certain ends being given, how shall these be most successfully reached? What outline of form, which is not a fleshless skeleton, but a graceful contour, will completely include these and no more?

The plan which excludes a needed member, or adds a worthless one, in order that a notion of symmetry, of beauty, may be met, therein shows its weakness, and that it is destitute of that power which can successfully shape all means to its own purposes.

It would also follow from this principle that ornament is most successful when it is not solely ornament, — when it both discharges a useful part in the plan, and a beautiful part in the outstanding form. An architecture in which the boldness of outline is broken by idle members, possessed in themselves of no assignable purpose, must be greatly inferior to one whose very conception, in the variety of its offices and wants, has a duty and a station for everything which it employs. Ornament which lacks use lacks justification, and, though agreeable in itself, can render but a stammering reason for its presence. The less it is a constituent of the plan, the more it burdens and obscures that plan, and substitutes a medley for a method.

While no principle contains a more important truth,

it cannot in art be so far pushed as to be made perfectly applicable to all the details of ornamentation. It is sufficient if it has been strictly regarded in the outline. As the precise pattern of the parts is in itself of less importance, the rule somewhat relaxes its hold, and suffers a less obvious connection to exist between these and the end proposed. The embossing of a door may be of one or of another design, without effecting the object for which it is made.

This principle of subordination is akin to what Ruskin terms obedience. "While a measure of license is necessary to exhibit the individual energies of things, the fairness and pleasantness and perfection of them all consist in their restraint. Compare a river that has burst its banks with one that is bound by them, and the clouds that are scattered over the face of the whole heaven with those that are marshalled into ranks and orders by its winds. That restraint utter and unrelaxing can never be comely is not because it is in itself an evil, but only because when too great it overpowers the nature of the thing restrained, and so counteracts the other laws of which that nature itself is composed. And the balance wherein consists the fairness of creation is between the laws of life and being in the things governed, and the laws of general sway to which they are subjected; and the suspension or infringement of either kind of law, or, literally, disorder, is equivalent to and synonymous with disease; but the increase of both honor and beauty is habitually on the side of restraint, or the action of superior law, rather than of character, or the action of inferior law. Exactly in proportion to the majesty of things in the scale of being is the completeness of their obedience to the laws that are set over them. Gravitation is less quickly, less instantly obeyed by a grain of dust, than it is by the sun and moon, and the ocean falls and flows under influences which the lake and river do not recognize. So, also, in estimating the dignity of an action or occupation of men, there is perhaps no better test than the question, Are its laws strict?"

It is finely taught in this passage, that, while even the freedom of beauty is obedience, the highest beauty lies in obedience to the highest law. The ease and power which we wish to see in any given object are not found in the waywardness, the obstinate rigidity, of the material, but in the mastery of a formative thought, before which everything, while retaining the integrity of its own qualities, is flexible, pliant, and apt.

The principle of subordination is not less controlling, when the end proposed is moral, — is the expression of sentiment. Beauty is then dependent on the character of the sentiment, and the vigor with which it is uttered. The problem becomes, with the symbols at the disposal of the artist, to impart a certain moral state, to penetrate the work with given emotions. Provided these emotions are not themselves base, the beauty of the product will depend on the success of this undertaking, and subordination will now be that of the means to the governing feeling. In the individual expression of this end, in the severity with which all that is alien is excluded, success consists.

If no such law exists in the mind of the worker, all is unruled, unformed in the work. There is no vigorous wielding of agencies, no striking concurrence of things diverse; the best material loses its power, and the purest emotions conceal their worth. Ornament becomes ornate, fantastic, and extravagant. With no principle to control it, it knows not where to begin or where to end, it becomes obtrusive, changeable and detached, and art passes into stage effect, — a fanciful shifting of trinketries. The decay of an art which has arrived at any unusual excellence is wont to commence in an insubordination of ornament, ending in total confusion. The naked, the bald statement of a thought, is ever invigorating; the profuse luxury of a wanton, debilitating.

It is the subordination of beauty which constitutes the difference between art and fashion, rendering the one so permanent, and the other so fickle. There is no law, no obedience in fashion, and as it depends solely on novelty, it must be ever on the move in search of it. It is bound to incessant change by the very lawlessness of its changes. Obedience is allied to truth. Obedient art knows the limitations and laws of nature, under which it works, and obeys them.

Under this principle of subordination, we can best speak of congruity and propriety. Congruity is the weaker of the two terms, and implies an agreement among things. Propriety, on the other hand, is more properly employed in connection with persons, and expresses the suitableness of things and actions to stations and characters. Every strongly defined object is by this very fact fitted to make certain impressions, is possessed of a certain character. From the relation of such an object to surrounding things, there immediately arises the impression of agreement or disagreement in character, of congruity or incongruity.

The more individual and decided are the qualities of any object, the more sensible and vigorous is the law of congruity which it imposes. One of the stronger illustrations of this principle is seen in what are termed styles of architecture. In the same style there is a strong agreement of members and methods, — a marked concurrence of expression, — and this imposes on the architect a stern command not to depart from the style once adopted, to work under its laws, to show the affluence of its resources, the vigor of its devices, and its entire applicability to every part of the structure. Upon this cheerful acquiescence in the laws of a style must depend the degree in which it shall be developed, the bold, independent, and powerful character which it shall assume, its ultimate worth to art.

An incongruity among things nearly related, if striking, is humorous, bringing them into contempt; if slight, it simply serves to weaken the impression which they would otherwise make.

Propriety, it will at once be seen, establishes a firmer law, and one more inclusive of details than congruity. Man has more character than irrational objects, his actions and the things by which he surrounds himself stand in more immediate and vital connection with him, and there is in reference to them, not only a suitableness, but an obligation. A large part of the pleasure or pain which we receive from our fellow-men arises from the proprieties or improprieties which are connected with them, and the law of propriety is more immediately efficient in most communities than the law of morals. The decisions of public opinion, pronouncing actions appropriate or inappropriate, are more heeded than those of conscience, pronouncing them right or wrong.

Propriety in one sphere of its duty may be said to be

the police of morals. Public opinion, forced onward by the advance of morality, multiplies its restrictions, and what the individual conscience has long announced in vain is at length sent forth as a command by this tardy lawgiver of the multitude. The virtue of the few at length becomes the propriety of all. What is conceded with a strict reference to right is virtue; what is conceded to the opinions and feelings of men concerning the right is propriety. The offences which this police law deals with are more numerous, but not always less heinous, than those judged by the higher criminal law. In the progress of virtue, acts relating to moral questions, which once passed without censure, are first pronounced inappropriate, and afterward criminal. When deep convictions of the wrongfulness of any course of action belong to a few only, while on the part of the majority there is but a lazy and partial acquiescence, the severest censure which can be secured is that of an impropriety, forcing it from the more public places. When, however, these convictions take possession of the mass of men, the act is regarded no longer as inappropriate merely, but criminal, and is put under the ban of the statute.

Propriety, then, in reference to one class of questions, is a sort of half-way ground between virtue and vice, a street decency imposed by respectable citizens, the adumbration of right.

Besides these more important questions which mark a transitional state of virtue, and are subject to propriety as the police of morals, there are others which are committed to it as the police of manners. These are points which are deemed too trivial to involve any moral questions, yet not so trivial as to be matters of indifference. Methods of speech and movement, garments and premises, are of this class. These are thought to be more particularly questions of taste, while action in its bearings on character is reserved for morals. A division which separates the manifestations of character into serious and trifling, and assigns the latter to æsthetics, is false and offensive.

All acts, the greater and the less, which reveal the heart, are subject to the two omnipresent and vital laws of rational life, — beauty and right. Beauty is as broad as is spontaneous obedience to appropriate law, whether this obedience, as rendered in the form of action, be termed propriety, or, as rendered in the inherent character of action, be termed virtue.

The lesser improprieties of life are objects of humorous or serious contempt; the greater, of scorn and disgust. It is evident, that while mere propriety, presenting so loose and easy a law, cannot go far to secure beauty, its want must at once be observable and highly disagreeable.

There is one direction in which art has indulged itself in a most marked violation of propriety, and that, too, on the side of vice. I refer to the frequent nudity of its figures. This is a point upon which artists have been pretty unanimous, and disposed to treat the opinions of others with hauteur and disdain, as arising at best from a virtue more itching and sensitive than wise, from instincts more physical than æsthetical. This practice has been more abused in painting than in sculpture, both as less needed and hence less justifiable, and as ever tending to become more loose and lustful in the double symbols of color and form, than when confined to the pure, stern use of the latter in stone or metal. Despite alleged necessities, — despite the high-toned claims and undisguised contempt of artists, — our convictions are strongly against the practice, as alike injurious to taste and morals. Indeed, if injurious to morals, it cannot be otherwise than injurious to taste, since art has no more dangerous enemy than a lascivious, perverted fancy. The grounds of our opinion we shall briefly render.

(*a.*) This practice violates the law of propriety. The assertion does not beg the question, for propriety is not established by art, — is not a law which it gives itself, but rests on the convictions of men, and passes into a recognized and governing principle in the actions of daily life. Propriety is an external law, in obedience to which beauty is realized, and not the notion of this or that artist, or of all artists.

Propriety comes from life to art, there to control its imitative forms and representative facts. A rule of propriety is an induction of the customs of life, brought to art as a principle by whose acceptance alone it can be either pure or true. If propriety were arrived at by seeing what has been found in art itself, it could constitute no guide to art, and the question of the propriety or impropriety of any practice would only be one of fact, whether it has or has not been prevalent. Our assertion, then, is true, that this practice is an impropriety, a violation of the settled law of life in all intelligent and Christian communities. If justified at all, it must be justified as an impropriety, as a direct violation of the most obvious law of decency and morals in social life. Has art then a right to establish a standard of its own, and to violate in favor of its supposed ends any principle it may please of decency and morals established by the healthy sense and virtue of men? Such an assertion at once sunders art from life, and makes it the most formidable antagonist of truth and right. Nor is it sufficient to say that this restraint of garments is the requisition of a fastidious custom, and indicates more of guilt than innocence.

Doubtless this is true as between a pure and chaste, and a sinful and licentious race, but not as between the different races of men. Human virtue is a virtue of garments and protections, and it avails not to say, that to the pure all things are pure, while men remain impure. As a matter of fact, — and this is a question to be decided not by art but by the exigencies of life, — all chastity has protected itself, has fortified itself with garments, and the clothed races are the virtuous races. Nor is the difficulty removed by the often repeated and pretentious affirmation, that art in herself is too vestal and high-souled to be affected, or suffer her votaries to be affected, by ordinary considerations. We meet this with a flat denial. The mass of men are to gaze on great art, and it is simply contrary to facts to affirm that in them all lower feelings are overborne by the pleasure of taste. The question is not alone concerning the purity of the statue, of the emotions which it was designed to arouse, but also of the emotions which it may arouse. If to the pure all things are pure, to the impure all things are impure, and at the breach in the law of propriety which we make in the name of virtue, there will troop in the lascivious imagery of an uneasy, omnipresent passion. It is a pretty fiction of poetry to speak of the nudity of art as "clothed on with chastity"; but we may well remember that it first applied this language to nude life.

Nor is it true, that art itself is so pure as to have nothing to fear. It has more than once been the base pander, the very pimp of lust. How are we to know that art is pure, unless it shows itself pure in its products?

In this world, at least, the best proof of purity is not a prurient desire to break through ordinary restraints, and walk with uncontrolled license. Such art may be pure, but its purity needs to be proved, not affirmed.

(*b.*) The source of this practice is against it. It is Grecian, pagan, in its origin. Because the art of Greece has kindled our own, it does not thereby follow that a Christian people are to adopt entire the art of an idolatrous and licentious people. If Christian sentiment and feeling can find adequate expression in old, and, in many of the conceptions which gave rise to it, corrupt art, such a fact is a most powerful and destructive argument against Christianity. We scorn a Christian art which has nothing more noble to say than a Greek mythology, whose worship was often but a Bacchanalian revel. It should also be remembered that Grecian customs were both a reason for, and a protection against, this practice, while ours in both respects are the reverse.

The Grecians were accustomed to the naked athlete, and had a right, which our artists and critics have not, to know the nude human form. Our artists reach their knowledge second-hand or surreptitiously, and then flaunt it against decency. Modesty urges the inquiry, How is the preliminary knowledge requisite to nude art acquired? The Greek custom had pronounced it decent to exhibit the naked human form, and their art at least was consistent, and violated no propriety which they had recognized in their social life. The forerunner of nude art with us ought to be nude life. Then should we both know the truth, and be armed against the temptation of our art. As things now are, the more strict is our daily habit, the more shocked and tempted we are by the startling indecency of our paintings and statues. We establish in life customs which keep us sensitive, and then indulge an art which plays upon that sensitiveness. We tamper with temptation, and have neither the innocence of nudity, nor the guarded virtue of garments. We make our art a lure, and spread it as a concealed net. Such a method must react to break down the law of propriety which it violates, or show itself in individual evil, in the morbid passion which it quickens.

The Grecian induration of custom is better than a Christian virtue which is employed only to keep us alive to the temptation of its lascivious imagination.

(*c.*) Facts are against this practice. The nudity of Grecian and Italian art in part sprang from, and in part occasioned, the licentiousness of those communities. Nude art, the world over, comes forth from a libertine atmosphere, and has only skulked with partial sufferance in pure communities. The whelmed cities of Pompeii and Herculaneum bear startling evidence of lust in art, conceived and finished. It is also true that our own communities, in proportion to the purity and elevation of their training, are startled by nude work, and gaze upon it with something of shame and silent guilt. A circle of ladies and gentlemen voluble and free in such a presence betokens either little modesty or great practice. This first jar and wound of a sensitive nature tell the whole story of guilt and of evil.

(*d.*) The subjects chosen for such art condemn it. They are more frequently a Venus, an Apollo, a Greek slave, some scrap of mythology, some remote historical or wholly ideal character. The conception of the artist must wander forth from present Christian and historic life to pick up and retouch the faded figures of a faith most justly forsaken, to waste its powers in again realizing the licentious goddess of love, or god of war, struggling, as the highest office of our Christian inspiration, to infuse a slight flush into these thrice dead and corrupt bodies, or to reach its own better notions in some form which, after all, to cover its nudeness, it must baptize with a classic or unreal name. It cannot introduce its naked savage as apostle or martyr, as general, councillor, or poet, but hides it in the darkness of licentious fiction or barbarous fact, or of ideal nothingness.

Why will not sacred subjects, historic subjects — the highest themes of art — suffer this treatment? Not less because it is against decency, than against truth. We violate truth by rendering Washington in the flowing robes of a Grecian, but no artist has been so bold as to render him nude, and chiefly because of the manifest outrage of such an act on virtue. We may be thought to misapprehend the office of nude art, in drawing an argument against it from the fact, that it cannot enter the historic field. It may be insisted that there yet remains for it a place in the ideal world. So far as ideal art works out its conceptions under a strictly human character and form, it must accept the same laws as art in its application to life. The ideal is here but the real purified and completed. Eve or a Greek slave must assuredly show their virtue in meeting the conditions of virtue in human life. When, however, as in the personification of morning, the ideal transcends the strictly human, and, on angelic wing, is poised between the earthly and heavenly, the law of propriety is of course modified, yet evidently not relaxed on the side of lust. Our ideal virtue should be not less virtuous than our life. The imagination may claim liberty, not license.

(*e.*) This practice has, we do not say, no justification, but no apology, in the necessities of art. Art does not need it, nay, is injured by it. From what has been said, we see that all its best themes will not suffer it. A Madonna, and not a Venus, a Christ, and not a Hercules, the history of its country, and not the fables of the dead, should be its ambition, and these precincts of virtue nudity dare not enter.

The face, the limbs, the frame, the attitude, are the grand organs of expression, the only organs of spiritual and intellectual expression. Nor are these so barren, so totally exhausted, that the curious artist must go elsewhere to find that which he may do, that which he may render.

All the concealed portions of the body are strictly physical in their adaptations and expression, and that taste which disciplines itself in rendering these will only be the more liable to lose the higher qualities of manhood, — to destroy the balance of godlike qualities on the side of the body, — to put muscle for will, softness for tenderness, and a full animal life for a vigorous, spiritual development. The argument from facts, both at this point and others, might be pushed much further, but the line of argument has been sufficiently marked out. The most entire and unquestioning obedience of beauty to virtue is her only safety.

More extended observation has convinced me of the justness of the views above presented, especially at two points, — the national debasement that comes with nude art, and the injury to art itself in its highest qualities. A distinguished American artist who had resided in Rome for twenty-five years said to me, "The Italians are nasty, filthy, beastly, in morals, as in body." Nude art may not be the cause of this, but is certainly its concomitant. Most of the European cities have a street decency that we should term indecent, and that is quite in keeping with the exposure of their art.

Christian art has manifestly suffered in its moral power and expression from a desire to secure striking physical attitudes and a fine anatomy. The Slaughter of the Innocents, the Judgment, and many other ever-returning themes, are often, in the handling, but little more than a complicated coil of human bodies and limbs, presenting, indeed, every variety of exposure and struggle, but quite barren of moral interest. Even the events of the crucifixion are more than once made the occasion for an attitude, or a lesson in muscular development, while painfully deficient in the divine passion that belongs to them. The Christian artist easily passed from a Madonna to a Venus, and repaid himself for the restraint of the one by the license of the other; while Susanna presented as a subject a midway ground of indulgence, of which he constantly availed himself. We shall hardly miss in any gallery of art this lustful story of the Apocrypha.

LECTURE IX.

ECONOMY OF BEAUTY. — REASONS FOR ECONOMY. — DIGNITY OF BEAUTY. — CHOICE OF THEMES. — TREATMENT OF THEMES. — SUMMATION.

THE second principle which we present, as controlling the manifestations of beauty, is its economy. Beauty, from the nature of the case, from the character of the objects in which it exists, and the faculties on which it operates, is subject to certain limitations. It may not be in full variety and high degree everywhere, but is amenable to laws of distribution and restraint, the observance of which may be called the economy of beauty.

The first of these restraints arises from the limited number of thoughts which can be received, of feelings which can be entertained, by the human mind in a given period. Finite faculties, as those of man, grasp at any one instant but little, and this little must be retained beyond the instant, that it may either be fully understood or felt. The fact that each emotion distinctly realized occupies time, and is slowly excluded by other emotions, gives to feeling what may be termed its natural flow, essentially the same for all, though somewhat accelerated or retarded by the active or sluggish temperament of the individual. If feelings are made to succeed each other more rapidly than is the habit of the mind, the faculties may for a short time be quickened and aroused, but they soon tire of objects the rapidity of whose movement wearies and bewilders them, and confusion, uneasiness, listlessness, and pain succeed. The mind determines itself to a certain rate of motion, and will not, for any length of time, accept with pleasure a movement either more or less rapid than its own. Fatigue and loss of interest are equally referable, either to more or less than can be readily apprehended. The heart is free, and can neither be spurred or reined in its pleasures.

This principle sets limits to the variety and fulness of parts, to the multiplicity of details in beautiful objects. The unity must not only be complete, but also level to the mind which is to enjoy it, including no more than its faculties can group and relate with that ease which constitutes pleasure.

The more disciplined the powers, the more full the variety which they will be capable of enjoying; and this growth of capacity is met in nature in two ways.

(*a.*) Detached portions of complex objects are in themselves beautiful, and may occupy the mind to the exclusion of remaining portions, or, as its grasp is enlarged, it may apprehend objects in broader and yet broader relations, travelling slowly up to a universe.

(*b.*) In the same object — as the human face — variety at first includes only its leading traits, and afterward, by study and increased knowledge, multiplies and enlarges itself on the same ground; even as the animal world, exhausted by the natural eye, has strata below strata of life awaiting the microscope. This principle is of constant application in art, demanding that, in the members of a building, the portions of a garden, the parts of a painting, there should not be a luxuriance so unpruned as to overgrow and conceal the outlines of order, — as to task the apprehension.

A second application of this principle is to transitions. Feelings do not follow each other in sharp outline, as black and white in trim mosaic, but tardily and unconsciously, as the blended colors which the sun melts into a cloud, or the vital force, into a tinged petal. Akin to this should be the steps by which the emotions glide onward. This is well illustrated by the effect of architecture on gardening. The one deals more with straight, the other with curved lines; and the freedom of the weaker art is somewhat lost as it approaches the dwelling, the representative of a stronger art. Everything begins to show the neighborhood of a sterner law; the paths become more direct, the shrubbery more closely cut, and an increasing utility is everywhere present. The one art influences the other, and only as the mind by distance begins to escape the trim circumspection of architecture, do the restrictions laid upon nature relax, and she once more shows to the full her careless, native ease. Transitions occupy both time and space. The mind refuses to vault from feeling to feeling at the will of the artist.

A second principle of economy arising from the limited capacity of the mind is, that a high degree of beauty — indeed, any beauty — is not always desirable. There are feelings which adequately occupy the mind without giving rise to this emotion, and feelings which give rise to it in very unequal degrees, according to the excellency of the objects which excite them. The demands of utility may be of such a nature as to render beauty unnecessary and impossible; and even from so favorite a feeling the mind is willing to find rest. Many awkward and disagreeable and loathsome objects, in their stern, stubborn truthfulness, have much more power to nerve and discipline the mind, than any mere varnish and gloss of an affected and superficial beauty. The heart is not to be enervated with a diet of perpetual pleasures.

Another fact, furnishing a third principle of economy to art, is, that some emotions, as similar, readily coexist and blend with each other, and that others, as dissimilar and opposite, exclude each other. Kindred emotions may be multiplied without destroying the unity of effect, and the mind passes from one to another of these with direct and ready transition. On the other hand, diverse feelings, tending mutually to weaken and destroy each other, cannot coexist except in skilful and limited contrasts, and the passage from one to another of these must occupy more time and include more steps. The first give rise to comparison, capable of a most broad and frequent application; the second, when the diversity becomes opposition, to antithesis, — of more rare and difficult use.

A fourth limitation to the impressions which the mind, from its very constitution, is capable of receiving, arises from the different duration and degrees of singleness in stronger and weaker feelings. The deeper the emotion, the less the time which it tends to occupy, and the more exclusive is it of all other feelings while it remains. The weaker the feeling, on the other hand, the longer the time it may occupy, and the less exclusive the possession which it takes of the mind. All higher forms of beauty, therefore, more especially those which are sublime, can only be of rare occurrence, while objects of more subdued expression will be repeated everywhere. The heart has, as habitual pleasures, the more moderate, and only seeks the occasional

stimulus of stronger enjoyments. There are ordinary as well as extraordinary states, and the last must always be few as compared with the first. The fiction which is extraordinary throughout loses not less its hold on truth than on the more just and common sympathies of the soul. There is little beauty unusual and striking, there is much familiar and commonplace, and that is the most healthy action of the mind which delights in ordinary objects, and finds in this homely fare adequate nourishment.

This principle also makes evident the more severe unity of treatment which a strong passion requires, and the greater variety which the milder feelings court. Quantity and quality are in inverse ratio. Fancy repeats her figures with more or less rapid succession throughout her patterns, and atones for their single insignificance by their joint effect. A fine statue or noble painting will not suffer repetition, and stands in its collected, individual worth, more worthy than if renewed in every niche, or on every wall.

For this reason, also, is it that, when a strong effect has once been produced, all further details or ornament must either be omitted or fall into the background, that the object may stand unobscured in the singleness of its principal power; and that, on the other hand, an object, as a landscape or building, by nature somewhat monotonous and uniform, demands the relief of ornament, and makes up for the paucity of original impression by an accumulation of details. There results from this characteristic of mind a strict economy of material.

Two strong effects cannot coexist. The heart, being filled with one object, rejects the second, and if it finds it forced upon it, is pained by the intrusion. The mind tends to temperance in its enjoyments. One strong pleasure satisfies it, nor will it long indulge this, but quickly returns to the frugality of weaker feeling.

Nor is this moderation and restraint of power, this chastity of the soul in its indulgences, characteristic of the weaker, but of the stronger and more self-contained spirit. There are ever in vice and ignorance a certain prodigality and extravagance of enjoyment. They squander all that they have at every entertainment; they plunge at once into the utmost expenditure, as if this were all too little. Their feast is a debauch; their garments, dyed deep in most positive colors, become fantastic finery. They engulf their daily pleasures in the extravagance of an hour; they waste their substance in riotous living. Nor does this arise from a quick appetite, an acute taste, a ready relish of enjoyment, but from faculties so rude that their stupid search of pleasure is ever breaking out into revel and riot. Of satisfaction, of the repose of pleasure, such persons know little or nothing.

On the other hand, virtue and knowledge, while affluent in resources, are ever characterized by a certain moderation in their use. There is in them a restrained power, a reserve more faithful and reliable even than the troops in the field, — a happiness which flows quietly on with its deep waters and its shallow, its long reaches of level and its occasional rapids. The divine power finds everything within its reach, yet there is in its movements nothing eccentric, extravagant, and startling, but all that is moderate, measured, patient, and even commonplace. Nor does this economy of pleasure which belongs to virtue and knowledge spring from any want of acuteness in feeling, but the reverse

Not only has the intelligent mind, as occupied with real and weighty interests, the hourly satisfaction incidental to its pursuits, but it discerns in familiar objects, which ignorance overlooks, so much, that it takes more pleasure in tarrying upon them than in being hurried on in the quest of novelty. It needs no stimulus, it waits for no excitement. It is not compelled, like some poor rogue, to do a violence, to waylay its pleasures with sword and pistol. It is rich, it has enjoyments on every hand, and so healthy and keen an appetite as to make a little a feast. The world unseen does more for it than for the eyes of another, and there is ever stealing in, it knows not how, as through an open lattice-work, the fragrance of distant flowers, the warmth and odor of distant fields.

An economy of beauty, then, is imposed upon us by the very poverty and limitation of our faculties, and is also the cheerfully accepted law of the thoughtful and fruitful mind.

A third not less important principle is the dignity of beauty. By dignity is here meant the intrinsic worth and power of an object, — the kind and degree of feeling which it is capable of expressing. There is no true dignity in nature aside from man, for in him alone is concentrated real worth, moral worth; yet, as many objects reflect for him intellectual and moral qualities, these have a worth greater or less according to the nature and fulness of these qualities, and a dignity which is the reflection of the dignity of their Author. By the dignity of beauty as a compendious principle of art, is meant the concurrence of intrinsic worth with merit of execution, the union of beauty in form with beauty in fact, the perpetual recollection that this high quality has intimate connection with interior qualities, and can only exist in a high degree as resting on a basis of substantial merit. The dignity of beauty is closely connected with what has already been said of beauty in expression. We there saw that beauty springs from a creative, a formative, an organic thought, and that all retreat, decay, and disease are not beautiful. That which has in it no advance of truth, no intrinsic worth, not less in the spiritual than in the physical world, has no dignity, and hence no basis for beauty. To the mind that apprehends vice as the retreat of virtuous life, — the defeat of spiritual strength, — there is in it that which puts beauty to flight, and so far, therefore, as an object presents itself as unworthy, it loses beauty, and there is no opportunity to humble true beauty in the correct presentation of vice. Indeed, few truths need so severe, or are capable of so impressive and instructive treatment, as the action of moral deformity on physical beauty, as the sack and ravage of a spiritual disease upon a goodly nature. It is evident that just here, also, there is the possibility of a most deep and damning lie, in the telling of which beauty shall lose all its dignity, all its worth. If vice is suffered to disguise itself, and wear a pure and regal beauty unstained by its own nature, the great fact of vice working itself out in deformity is kept back. Beauty as much becomes a lusty paramour as a pure vestal. Wherever the desertion of right is not presented as the desertion of beauty, art is degraded, and disgraced by the companionship of vice, and with the vileness of her own ministrations reflects scorn on the beauty which she courts.

The principle of dignity, of worth, also comes in as

a guide in the treatment of objects possessed of different degrees of intrinsic value. It does not suffer the artist to bestow equal labor and affection on all kinds of work, or upon all parts of the same work, but compels him to a perfect understanding of character, that just themes may be chosen, that strong points may be made to stand out in their relative proportions, that a right respect may be rendered to intrinsic worth, and that beauty may receive dignity from the justness of its awards and the merit of its favorites. This principle governs both in the choice and treatment of themes. Only certain objects are capable either of calling out or of receiving the highest enthusiasm, — the best skill. At this point worth is closely allied to truth. Those objects which contain the most and the most important truths, which have themselves been the largest recipients of divine thought, have for man the greatest worth, and should have over him the greatest power. The mere correctness of a representation is not a sufficient guaranty of its merit. There remains among truths the opportunity of choice, and the general character of its selections will decide the character of any art.

(*a.*) Themes are determined as higher and lower by the purity and power of the expression which they severally contain. Man and human history may at once be the highest and lowest objects of art, according as developed on the side of heroic strength, or sensuous indolence, — according as rendered in the rareness of that which is possible, or in the deep vulgarity of that which is too often actual. Aside from anything perverted and false, which is now excluded, there is yet in man the widest range of topic, corresponding to the sweep and grasp of his nature, and, therefore, that which is both more and less worthy of elaborate skill. Wasted power is here very closely allied to perverted power.

Animate nature, with a full catalogue of secondary truths, furnishes a lower, and yet a safer, field of art. Much good work, and even great work, though not the greatest, can be done in the adequate representation of animal life. The landscape and natural scenery, in the unalloyed purity, delicacy, and power of the emotions to which they give rise, in the intense and broad sympathy with God's work which they imply, will ever furnish permanent objects for the most thoughtful and emotional art. Indeed, an intense love of nature, though it seems in part a desertion of the higher for the lower, of the moral for the physical, yet largely atones for this, in the strengthening tone and purity of its feeling, and more often marks the growth than the decay of taste. Among various objects open to its pen, pencil, and chisel, the dignity of art will show itself in the fulness of the theme, in its refusing to tarry on that which is lower, and measuring its strength with that which is highest.

(*b*.) Some truths are accidental, others general; some individual, others specific and generic; some grotesque and odd, others strangely typical and characteristic. It is the second class of representative facts which has importance, which is strictly true to nature, marking her laws and tendencies. These may have less of mere novelty, but they have much more of real excellence; less of that extravagance which startles and pleases for the moment, but much more of that wisdom and law which mark the workings of true power. It is these only which have the worth, the dignity, of a system, and a method, and which therefore deserve the elaborate presentation and perfect completion belonging to that which lies in the very line of order, and represents the workings of a living force, of a power perpetually creative of kindred products. It is not the accidents, but the purposes, of nature which have interest. That which is perfect in any kind of life, though most rare, is not therefore akin to the anomalous and the accidental, but is rather the complete realization of law, — the fullest utterance of that which is.

(*c.*) Truth attaches an additional value, an additional dignity, to historic work, — to the presentation of Christian facts, beyond that which belongs to vague mythological conceptions, — to the portraying of national heroism, beyond that of ideal virtue. The different arts are quite distinct from each other in the length of time required to mellow facts into appropriate themes for their efforts. Painting may lay hold of recent events, and still find full play for its combining and creative imagination. It is true within fixed limits, yet these, far from unduly constraining, may often supply a most wholesome and needed law to its efforts.

Poetry, on the other hand, thrown back more on the naked narrative, the bare fact, is thought to be forced of necessity into a region of fiction. So far, undoubtedly, it loses something of value, — a loss for which it can only find compensation by making its fiction most thoroughly and broadly presentative of facts. Indeed, the success of much modern poetry would seem to show that this desertion of the actual is not necessary.

The principle of dignity has more control in the treatment than in the choice of a theme.

(*a.*) All that is odd and fantastic, that is mere conceit, that has in it no basis of fact, is thereby excluded.

A most striking illustration of this maltreatment is sometimes furnished in gardening. Trees and shrubs are trained and clipped into mathematical figures, into cones and pyramids, or some remote resemblance of animal forms. This is one of the most foolish rebukes man has ever given to nature, and deserves to be followed by, Get behind me, Satan. To cut and shear the character of a plant all away from it, and to put in place of its native, free, and varied outline, its new and individual life, some scrap of mathematics taken from the lower, the inorganic and mechanical world, shows a mind oddly out of sorts with truth and God. A trained hedge is only justifiable on the ground of utility, and in its use may be more beautiful than if left wild. An ornamental shrub or tree, on the other hand, is planted for its native power, and all right training will only develop this. To make it forget its God-ordained message, and repeat forever, as with parrot tongue, our stupid wits, is a species of profanity. Another example of remote and valueless resemblance is furnished by worsted work and kindred products of female indolence. These, simply because they have deserted the province of use, *do not become* beautiful. Subject to the same condemnation are the word-tricks of poetry, by which quaint expression is made to do the work of true feeling, by which familiar thoughts, hidden in the folds of a new guise, elude old friends like revellers at a masked ball.

(*b*.) Dignity excludes the use of unworthy material in the arts. The durability of oil paintings gives them a superior dignity as compared with water-colors, and the difference between the statue in marble and its model in plaster lies largely here. This also condemns wax-work, and reduces the best-executed artificials to trivial ornaments.

(*c.*) Dignity also determines what part of the work shall receive the highest execution. The noblest figure in the painting must command the best skill of the artist, and the touch of the pencil must nowhere be so perfect as to draw away the attention. The rich folds of the garment are not to stand between the spectator and him who wears it, unless by design we mark the rank and station as more than the man: the flower in the foreground is not to be more attractive than the main effect. In architecture, nearness in position and proximity to leading entrances impart worth to members, and therefore demand increased delicacy. Height and distance, on the other hand, suffer the workman to cut with a more bold and careless chisel. Allied to this dignity of members is the nature of the purpose for which any edifice is erected, and which at once determines its character and the degree of labor and ornament of which it is rightly susceptible.

On the constancy with which every modification of purpose results in a corresponding modification of structure will largely depend the variety and worth of a nation's architecture, the amount of character and feeling which it will reveal. Any style of architecture will show its power by its pliancy, its ability to meet the varied, multiplied demands laid upon it. A barn must honestly show its purpose, and cannot receive the labor and ornament of a dwelling without degrading them. A dwelling, the home of a citizen, has no right to the pretension of a palace. It is strictly private, and may not, in arrogant assumption, tower above its neighbors. It would thus become the expression of selfish ease, of ungenerous and offensive self-assertion. Fifth Avenue may mark as strongly the infamy of wealth as Five Points the infamy of poverty. No architecture can be beautiful when only showing the wide, hard, unpitying hand which the owner stretches abroad to gather into his own cormorant-nest the goods and enjoyments of the world, the high and the sharp paling with which he fences in his own from another's, the cold, glazed eye with which he looks out on the suffering and want which are exiled from his own threshold.

The dignity of beauty restrains the individual in his architectural not less than in his personal outlays. The dignity of a nation renders appropriate a massive magnificence, a mastery of material and time that leave durable and deeply wrought traits of character on all that it does.

The subordination of beauty gives us its relation to other things, the method of its presence, as arising from the subservience of the object to some ulterior end, or from the relation of parts within the object. Economy of beauty gives us the limitations to which it is subject, — the conditions which restrict its presence. The third principle — the dignity of beauty — shows us where it may be present, what objects may, under the form of obedience and when not excluded by a just moderation, receive it.

The three principles of subordination, economy, and dignity may be said to answer the three questions, How? How much? and Where? and thus together, if adequately answered, to constitute a complete guide to action. There is one further question of guidance and criticism answered in previous lectures, and that is, What ends as brought out in any object — what kinds of expression — are beautiful. This point being settled, and there being present that in the creative thought, in the controlling purpose, which renders the work capable of beauty, it remains to examine the product in reference to the perfect control which this thought has everywhere exerted, the restraint and moderation everywhere shown in its ornament, and the fitness of the points at which the more elaborate work is displayed. That these principles mutually sustain each other, and therefore in some degree involve each other, will readily be seen. Nor does this prevent their furnishing distinct criterions of judgment. That object is the most beautiful in whose execution there is the sternest obedience, the most wholesome restraint, the most accurate gradation of worth.

LECTURE X.

THINGS WHICH MISLEAD TASTE.—NOVELTY.—AN INFERIOR QUALITY.—RESEMBLANCE.—ASSOCIATION.—HABIT.—CUSTOM.

WE have pointed out the principles which guide taste, and now wish to direct attention to some of the things which mislead it. First among these is novelty. The mind is so constituted, that things strange and unusual in form or action immediately attract its attention, and fill it with the feeling of wonder. This feeling is of itself pleasurable, besides the advantage which belongs to it of being so quickly able, to the exclusion of other emotions, to take possession of the mind. Novelty is often associated with beauty, and we may confound the effect of one quality with that of the other. The artist, too weak to reach true beauty, may strive to supply its place with novelty,—with that which is strange, and thus striking. This effort, when momentarily successful, must always fail of reaching any permanent result,—must fall greatly short of beauty.

There are certain things which mark novelty as an inferior quality, for which no valuable quality is to be sacrificed,—as capable only of an immediate and vulgar effect, and not worth the slightest sacrifice of intrinsic merit.

(*a*.) The emotion to which it gives rise is necessarily transient. Familiarity robs every object of its novelty, and, if it has no better qualities, leaves it in the long catalogue of neglected commonplaces. An emotion whose very realization is its inevitable, its almost immediate destruction, shows itself possessed of only a transient, secondary office.

(*b.*) Novelty as a quality is due to our ignorance, and not to our knowledge. It is strictly negative. It looks to nothing belonging to the object, to no intrinsic merit, but merely to our want of previous acquaintance with it. It is therefore rather an accidental and passing relation of things than a quality. It consists equally with the absence of merit as with its presence, and in proportion to our ignorance will play be given to novelty and the induced feeling of wonder.

Springing, therefore, as it does, from so unimportant a circumstance as our want of previous knowledge, novelty indicates nothing permanent in itself, or of permanent interest. The more thoughtful the mind, the more it moderates and restrains its wonder, both as a tacit confession of ignorance, and also of a mind that has not yet rightly apprehended the universal strangeness of things even the most familiar.

(*c.*) Novelty possesses little value for the philosophical mind, because it is not in that which is accidental, strange, or diverse that it finds its most important lessons. It inquires rather into agreements and resemblances, since these mark the presence of principles, and are the paths of law.

Discrepancies and disagreements have no especial value except as interpreted by agreements, and the mind that is in search of broad truths and inclusive statements is in search of commonplaces rather than novelties. The radical harmony of the one has for it more interest than the transient variety of the other.

(*d.*) Novelty and the wonder to which it gives rise are also disparaged by association with a vagrant, prying, and sometimes mischievous curiosity, which, with greedy appetite, seeks for the news, with no heed of the worthlessness of the garbage which is thrown to it. An earnest inquirer after truth, seeking what is, and not what is new, has no sympathy or partnership with the gossip of a newsman, or the heed that waits with ears ajar on a novelty-vender. Curiosity, as wakefulness to that which is unknown, indicates a mind alive to knowledge, — as wakefulness to that which is new, it indicates the weariness of a heart, that, in the dull drudgery of its insipid pleasures, has worn out, and is worn out by, the old.

Novelty, then, is both legitimate and illegitimate, — is present in the highest and weakest art. The creations of genius are brought out with surprising freshness, and yet they are but the carrying out and completion of that which was known, — a magnificent application of familiar laws, — a new development of the power and adaptations of method. They are ingrafted, by the whole strength of their controlling principle and interior life, upon the old, and, as the sap of the former root flows up into them, it comes within the reach of a new vital force, which, working with fresh intensity, brings forth a strangely superior product.

The novelty, on the other hand, which marks a decay of power is extravagant, taking the place of law, not revealing it, removing the familiar, not illustrating it, startling the mind, not instructing it. It awakens us as if to attention, and yet has nothing worth the while to say. It exists in perpetual struggle with the indolence, forgetfulness, and oversight of a mind which is not moved by any permanent interest. It is an attempt to advertise that which is not worth the pains of the purchaser. The longer this is done, the more odd and the more unsuccessful will be the devices resorted to.

Dress calls for the action of taste, but has chiefly fallen under the dominion of fashion, with whose edicts taste has little to do. This has taken place under the action of two principles, novelty and association. The leaders in fashion seek for the distinction and attention to which novelty gives rise: those who follow in imitation find their tastes and desires at once warped and determined by the association of ideas, by the connection of the new fashions with those whom they regard as the gentry, whom they have chosen to make their *élite*. The one party — more independent, yet more meanly dependent — win attention by striking out from the path in which the masses have begun to follow. The other, servilely catching the new tastes and notions, make haste to conform their action, and share the honors of their illustrious leaders. Since, in the world of fashion, the more striking the novelty, the more effective is the movement, extravagance succeeds extravagance, often resting its success on its very violation of taste. Fashion may be said to be a systematized pursuit of novelty, and wherever it prevails, does so largely at the cost of comfort and taste.

Fashion may also be said to be the impotence of taste, substituting for the gratification of a higher intuition the meaner pleasures of wonder and novelty. As a community is capable of the better, it will desert the inferior impulse; as its ignorance debars it from the higher, will it fall into the lower pursuit.

The rule of fashion is not to be recognized so far as it can be successfully resisted; but this resistance cannot proceed to all degrees. Fashion establishes a transient usage, which, through familiarity, is made more or less agreeable, and will certainly be unobtrusive. The unfashionable, on the other hand, being in a measure unusual, is somewhat obtrusive, and exposes itself to comment. Sheer modesty, therefore, may sometimes drive one into the protection and obscurity of fashion, or, at least, limit his violation of it. For this reason, much is resigned to fashion which could otherwise be better ordered. While dress and furniture are the chief, they are not the exclusive, field of fashion. It has much to do with the fine arts, — with the kind of use to which they are for the moment put, and the nature and measure of the admiration which they temporarily receive. As the principles of taste present in art become stronger, proportionately authoritative, and capable of perfect guidance, so fickle and false an arbiter should be carefully excluded. It is fashion which now plants all evergreens, and now plucks them all up; now fills every nook with statuettes, and now neglects them.

A second consideration, which often embarrasses and misleads the judgments of taste, is resemblance. The mere agreement of one thing with another, perfection of representation, is not beauty, though fitted to give the mind pleasure.

A likeness, according to the original character of an object, may or may not be beautiful; but if a perfect likeness, it will still afford some satisfaction, arising from the skill exhibited by the artist. The pleasure springing from beauty is to be carefully distinguished from that which belongs to successful imitation. The one depends on the intrinsic power of the object, whether a copy from nature or the creation of the mind; the other has no connection with the object, provided only it be fitted to tax the skill. An anatomical painting may impart as much of the pleasure which arises from resemblance as the finest portrait. The one depends on the intuitive and creative power of the artist, by which he seizes and utters expression; the other on the care with which he observes, and the skill with which he repeats particulars.

Beauty and resemblance are not concurrent in their aims, pleasures, or means. The first is never, like the second, indifferent to the object on which it employs its art, and the object being chosen, it strives rather to repeat and renew its power than faithfully to transcribe it. The highest resemblance is not always the most complete success, even when the object represented is beautiful. The treatment which deceives the senses does not employ precisely the same qualities and characteristics as that which gives the expression, and addresses the reason. Beauty makes a study of leading and pregnant truths; resemblance, of marks and coincidences which, though prominent to the senses, may be intrinsically of slight value.

Many of the less significant points which mark the man may be carefully given, and make the portrait a successful likeness, while the higher qualities which reveal and transfigure the manhood may be feebly rendered, and leave it an insignificant painting.

Resemblance, at best, gives only what physically is, and that through its more superficial and accidental tokens. Beauty sets the latent forces of the soul at work, and gives the face as the subject, instrument, and index of a spiritual life.

While art, therefore, as creative and beautiful, requires the attention to be directed to wholly other considerations than those by which a deception is played upon the senses, and has a distinct and much higher satisfaction to impart than that of resemblance, there is yet a manual skill and a certain careful observance of minor truths to be obtained by faithful copying. Success demands equally two elements, — creative, inventive power, and truthful, easy, and accurate representation, — a mastery of thoughts and of the means of expression. This knowledge of method can only be reached by practice, and much of this practice will be in the direction of faithful copying and representation.

The power of securing resemblance is greatly inferior to invention, and can never take its place. This difference is well brought out in the fact that the complete success of the one is often, as in fresco, a deception, a lie, and of the other a noble truth; the one misleads and confounds the senses, the other instructs the heart.

A third fact which, in its effect upon the taste, deserves attention, is the law of mental phenomena which we term association. Many things are deemed more or less beautiful, not from anything present in them, but from the associations by which they are connected with other things in the mind judging them. Nothing is long left wholly to its own intrinsic merits. It soon comes to have an acquired character, derived from the circumstances with which it has been connected, — a suggestion of times and places and purposes, — a reminiscence of things, agreeable or dis agreeable, which have stood in relation to it. This secondary character, these derived impressions, are different for different individuals, and are not readily separated in the mind's estimates from those qualities which make the object the same for all.

Associations of this sort rule the judgments of many, — we may almost say of the mass, — and a thing is deemed beautiful, not from what they have found in it or received from it, but from the position which they have seen it occupy in the world of wealth, or of art, or of opinion. Its merit is to them derived from its associations, and the moment it falls from the favor of the high, and becomes the antique fashion of a poor neighbor, the object of their former envy is now their laughter. They are alike heartless and brainless in both feelings.

Association is the reproductive power of the mind. It is through it that the past is perpetually renewing itself in the thoughts and imagery of the present. As the servant of memory, it restores the information committed to its arrangement and charge; as the servant of imagination, it brings forward the forms and truths of past experience to be wrought in the constituents of a new work; obedient to desire, it recalls former pleasures, and adds to the joys of the object and the hour the kindred joys of other years. As association draws upon the past, and only revivifies the scenes which our previous history has given it, the character and worth of its restored pictures must depend on their original value. Virtue has this additional reward, that the present is bound back by many chains of association to the virtuous and just pleasures of the past, and that it is ever summoning to its society these cheerful memories. No joy walks alone. No note of music is left to die away alone. The pleasures of the soul gather in groups, and troop forth in companies, each, by the very law of its presence, at harmony with its fellow.

Vice has this additional condemnation,—that the present is dogged and hunted down by the evil companionship of the past, that its words have the taint, and its suggestions the stain of a worn-out debauch, that it cannot shake itself loose from the foul memories which hang about it, nor rebuke the malignant and sneering devils now evoked even by the purest objects.

This aggregating, accumulating power of association, by which it intensifies every effect with the kindred experiences of the soul, shows itself at once in connection with beauty. The slightest things by association are endowed with the strength of the greatest. A flower becomes the harbinger of spring, and a single leaf or bough, as it deepens to scarlet, the token of autumn. The cultivated taste each hour lengthens its register of beauties, and each hour extends and strengthens the network of associations by which they are bound to each other and to a common service of pleasure.

In a carefully correct criticism of individual objects, the mind needs to be guarded against the warping power of previous association. This necessity may be inferred from the fact that all beauty has been referred to association. It also needs in the culture of taste to establish those just associations which shall enhance its enjoyments without misleading its judgments. An educated and virtuous taste has much to hope and little to fear from association, since this power only acts in the direction, and quickens the effect, of our past feelings and beliefs.

On the other hand, the associations which spring up in connection with a partial or neglected training are to be carefully questioned, and oftentimes overborne, by more just feelings and correct judgments. Of this sort is the aversion with which ignorance or prejudice regards many forms of animal and even human life. These lead to a total oversight of the admirable adaptations and striking beauty in them, and often give rise to a stupid cruelty, equally disgraceful to the heart and the intellect.

The person who diligently studies the various forms of healthy life, while confessing the relative feebleness of expression in some, can hardly fail to acknowledge the gracious wisdom, the beauty, appearing in all. With this enlarged observation of benevolence, there will spring up increasing and more inclusive love, and, through an appreciation of the beauty and excellency of the workmanship, the soul will be put in broader sympathy with the universe about it.

The debasing associations of ignorance and vice which chain down the spirit need to be broken before it can arise and fully receive the impressions of a world, wise, benevolent, and beautiful in all its native forms and methods.

The effects of association are sometimes so mingled with intrinsic qualities as not readily to be separable. It is often remarked, that those who are known to be good are thought to be beautiful, while an imperious and unpleasant character gives rise to an impression of ugliness. This is brought out in the proverb, "Handsome is that handsome does."

This opinion is not wholly due to association. Not only may we suppose that the expression of the face and the character of the indwelling spirit have originally some relation to each other, but the former is placed under the immediate control of the latter, and through the constant exercise of this influence ultimately assumes, in all its permanent and legible lines, the feelings and passions of the soul. No face can long resist or conceal its daily avocations. The constant organ of characteristic, individual expression, it is in repose neither silent nor untruthful. Its messages, like words that live in echo, reach the soul when the tongue is silent. The features, fading down into rest, do not wholly lose the passion that last played upon them. In the soul's sleep there is yet a twilight on the face that tells what the day has been.

As the countenance is in perpetual subjection to the soul, the feeling and opinion which we gradually attach to a face are more than mere association. They are interpretation, — a more correct and thorough apprehension of the peculiar signs which an individual spirit employs. Every soul does not signal the world in precisely the same method. Its muscular mechanism is not ever equally perfect, — its transparency equally pure, — its play of lip, nostril, and eye equally expressive. The way in which it manages its own instruments is in part to be learned. And not till the countenance, as subject to the various phases of thought, has been made familiar, can we altogether judge its power. This acquired, secondary character, by which the face of a friend is to us more than that of a stranger, may arise as much from our increased insight into the signs of character, from our enhanced power of interpretation, as from affection.

That association greatly aids in securing this result none can doubt; and the redemptive power of virtue, by which it conceals defects, quickens beauty, and makes the mind partial to its instruments, marks well its superior and pervading excellence.

The only consideration of which it remains to speak, as misleading the mind in its æsthetical judgments, or as liable to establish impressions adverse to good taste, is habit. This is distinct from fashion in the principle which gives rise to it, and in the manner of its action. The one springs from a love of the new and strange; the other, from a love of the old and familiar: change is with one the necessity of its existence, and stability with the other. Fashion is the result of the restless, uneasy temperament of the mind, by which it chafes with the fixed and orderly; habit, of its tendencies to settled attachments and fixed relations, as wearying of the perpetual ebb and flow of events. Youth in its volatility is most open to the influence of fashion: old age, averse to change, is the dependant and often the slave of matured habits. A fashion is strongest in its influence the moment it is realized, and thence rapidly declines; a habit is in its incipiency weak, and is from that point slowly but steadily confirmed in strength. Fashion is the jostle and confusion of the world, habit its retirement and tranquillity. The one is the radicalism, and the other the conservatism, of manners. The second demands more respect, and exerts a more even and permanent power than the first. Custom, which is the habit of a community, fortifies itself with antiquity, arms itself with the potent power of possession, and, inclosed within the double associations of the past and present, is firmly entrenched against change.

As far as art is representative it cannot be truthful without thoroughly understanding and recognizing the effect of habit, without adequately rendering this tendency of character to confine and conform itself to settled modes of action. So far as art is presentative, creative of that which is better and more beautiful, it has evidently occasion to test the claims of each habit, and, if it has no adequate support, to reject it and put over against it that which is able to justify itself to the taste and judgment. In things relatively indifferent, habit may furnish a convenient law; but to allow it to overawe or put down our better convictions is to give way to the chronic growl of a toothless conservatism, made only the more querulous by concession. As an illustration of the evil influence of custom, we may instance the stereotyped and meaningless form of much domestic architecture, the size and arrangement of yards, and the color of dwellings. A heavy, monotonously regular front, a small, rectangular enclosure, and glaring white, are what custom claims, and most are contented to secure.

The difference between habit and fashion is seen in the character of the things which they respectively most affect. Dress is the chosen field of the one, while buildings and the more permanent accompaniments of life are most influenced by the other. The term habit employed to designate one's garments, as a riding-habit, would seem to look back to a period less fickle in its fancies than our own.

It is evident that custom cannot be so violently and

strenuously resisted in æsthetics as in morals, since the one is ultimately a question of pleasure, and the other of duty. It may here sometimes be better to repress a principle than to provoke a prejudice, since it is not an abstract but a pleasurable expression of truth that is aimed at. Custom, when it has established a law for the protection of decency and morals, can most imperatively claim that it should be respected by art, that she should not, with her supposed exigencies, overrule the stern regulations on which rest the safe government of life.

If we distinguish custom and habit from each other, — as the one the usage, the law which the habits of the many have assigned the community, and the other, the method, the ever-returning mode which the action of the individual assumes, — it is evident that the first, through the stability, order, and protection which it gives to society, is closely allied to civil law, and will usually demand a much more cautious and circumspect treatment than the second. A custom may not so readily be violated or set aside as a habit. Both custom and habit exert a subtile influence over our judgments, concealing from us the defects of those things which they have sanctioned. They preoccupy the ground with strong feelings of their own. Many of the preferences to which they give rise are strictly prejudices, — prejudgments in favor of that which familiarity has rendered agreeable.

Habit weakens both pain and pleasure. That which is habitual addresses the feelings less strongly than that which is new, and our familiarity with objects, both repulsive and pleasant, has usually the effect to weaken the impression they make upon the feelings, and hence in part incapacitates the mind to judge them correctly. Habit begets a certain dulness of the faculties, by which they come more readily to endure protracted evil, and to experience less enjoyment from protracted pleasure, thus on either hand equalizing feeling, and softening down its intensities. Though habit, through this form of its action, ameliorates a condition of misery and poverty, and disappoints a spirit of selfish accumulation of its coveted pleasures, it is evident that it also weakens the hold of the feelings and judgment on the real character of things, and perverts our æsthetical and moral perceptions. Since habit, when once confirmed, confers no pleasure, but rather the reverse, it might be thought to be without adequate means of supporting its authority. Its rule is one of force, rather than of persuasion; of tyranny and the scourge, rather than of freedom and reward. Habit when violated has great power of inflicting discomfort, and the more unreasonable and pernicious the habit has been, the more severe and protracted is the penalty of pain with which its violation is usually visited. In this respect it is like the momentum of a body, which does not much show itself till an effort is made to check the motion; then it becomes deadly, and sends the ball crashing and bruising through all obstacles. Habit is often but the momentum of the body, or the heart, or the mind, impelled by which it runs along in a rut of indulgence or indolence, and cannot be lifted out.

Even where habit is on the side of virtue, in the very support which it renders the right, it is liable to make the soul's action more and more mechanical, — to leave it satisfied with a stolid repetition of the past, rather than to incite it to higher realizations, to bold and determined progress.

Habit, therefore, as tending to restrain the free judgments, and prejudice the taste, to mislead and weaken the feelings, and commit our active powers to the blind lead of worn-out precedents, needs to be most assiduously watched over and guarded against. Its dominion is everywhere, and all the chronic evils of life and art will be found sheltered and intrenched in habit and custom. Taste, like judgment, while reverencing and loving the past, must sometimes forget it, that it may meet with unbiassed heart the new conditions of the present. Yet habit rightly formed is the ease of confirmed virtue, the grace of good breeding, the adroitness of disciplined powers, the assurance of consolidated strength. Most to be feared and most to be sought, — the inflexible mould in which our life is ever cooling, the unchangeable pattern into which it is ever setting, — it demands momentary revision and watchfulness.

Of these misleading influences, association is, perhaps, the most powerful. It occasions in one a great distrust of the public taste and of the independent character of the æsthetical faculty to observe the fixed rounds which travellers pursue, their easy acquiescence in the stereotyped judgments of those who have gone before them, the insensible and unsensitive way in which they take up the praises custom assigns the several products of art, and the blind conventional form in which they pass them on to others. We hardly know which distresses us most, — the stolidity or the enthusiasm of these hasty disciples of art.

LECTURE XI.

LANDSCAPE GARDENING.—RELATION OF THE ARTS.—RIGHT OF CRITICISM.—DIMENSIONS OF GARDEN.—OBJECT OF GARDENING.—ITS RESOURCES, PLANTS, PLANTATIONS, NATURAL FEATURES, SURROUNDINGS, SPACES, WALKS, FENCES.—ARCHITECTURAL AIDS.—POWERS DISCIPLINED.

THE fine arts are six, and readily fall into three groups,—gardening and architecture, sculpture and painting, music and poetry. Gardening and architecture are united, not as giving play to the same powers or exciting the same feelings, but as often the accompaniments and complements of each other; architecture giving character to the grounds, and the grounds acting upon the architecture, and the two uniting in one effect. These arts, also, are pre-eminently controlled by utility, having immediate reference to the use and pleasure of occupants or owners.

Sculpture and painting are one in their impressions,—their relation to pleasure and gratified taste,—in the powers they call forth in the artist, and in their common elements of expression,—form and attitude.

Music and poetry are related both in the harmony of the emotions to which they give rise, and in the mutual aid which they render each other. Song is the combined power of music and poetry. The one supplies clearness and precision to emotion; the other, power and volume; the one gives direction, and the other impulse, to the soul.

In determining the relative rank of these arts, we consider the powers demanded and exercised by them in the artist; the scope and variety of their means; and the fulness of their presentations to the mind. So judged, we should arrange the groups, and the arts contained in them, in the order in which they have been already mentioned, commencing with gardening, and rising in the scale through architecture, sculpture, painting, and music, to poetry, the queen of arts.

Gardening reaches no higher than the lowest kingdom of life, and is there presentative, not creative. Its chief influence is due to the forces of vegetable life which work under its bidding. Architecture, throughout, is creative, owes its main power, not to that which it brings forward, but to its own skilful combinations, and in its ornamentation draws upon all living forms.

In passing to sculpture, we reach an art which directly and distinctively treats the human form, and the more subtile and spiritual beauty therein expressed. There is, to be sure, not the same breadth of invention, the same skill and fertility of resources, presented here as in architecture, but in the great requisite of beautiful expression, deep, various, and refined feeling, the art which makes man its subject has an advantage not to be compensated. There may be more reflection, more action of the intellect, but there is less intense beauty, less taste, in architecture than in sculpture. The task of the sculptor may be less varied, and call for less ingenuity, but it demands a nobler idea, a more thorough perception and spiritual insight than that of the architect. Painting includes the subject of sculpture and more, and presents its object not only in form and attitude, but also in shade and color. While it brings man forward as its chief theme, it has through the whole field of nature subordinate themes, full and quickening. Its range is commensurate with the visible universe, and all that enters our spiritual temple through its royal portal, its beautiful gate, the eye, may be presented in painting.

In passing to our third group, the subsidiary art of which is music, we seem, in one respect, to have fallen. The mind is now reached through its secondary avenue, the ear, and there is a loss — but partial, however — of that varied wealth which belongs to the eye. If music stood alone, this objection, we think, would be fatal to the rank here allowed it. But as the companion and partner of poetry, it retains its position by her side, and comes both to share and enhance her clearness and power of expression. Taking, then, poetry as the royal, the representative member of the group, we see its rank justified by the breadth of the field which belongs to it. It roams wherever imagination and feeling roam, and within the limit of the mind's faculties it is without limit. It includes in its images all that the other arts present, and much more. It is as reflective of all exterior and interior phenomena as the mirror of language. Content with no single, transient image on the shifting canvas of life, it gives the whole as a living experience, a continuous flow of vital forces. Not moments, not the pause of events, as to the painting, but periods, and the movement and hurry of forces, are intrusted to it. The poem is a series of landscapes, is the soul daguerrotyped in each successive hour of its existence with the full, changing play of light upon it, and of its impulses within it. While the painting renders a point in time, a cross-section of events, to the poem belongs continuous time, — the birth of actions, their growth, their epic and dramatic issue.

Nor is this — its fuller mastery of time — its only superiority; it has also a fuller mastery of space, of those objects at any one instant presentable in space. Its want of accuracy and completeness in detail, the relatively slender furniture of its pictures, enable it to move the more rapidly, to involve wider fields, and fields more remote from each other, and to multiply its scenes with a facility and wealth unattainable elsewhere. The supersensual character of its images enables it to treat many themes for which the touch of the brush is too rough. The angelic and divine, while yielding readily to the poet, may greatly embarrass or wholly elude the painter. The very fact that in poetry the imagination paints for the imagination, with no other medium than wholly arbitrary signs, gives a scope and boldness which cannot readily be reached in more accurate, and hence more sensuous images. Every man's imagination is addressed, stimulated, and directed by the poem, but not so definitely bound and straitened by the words as not to find large play for its own creative power. The painting, within its limits, does more for the eye, but by this very fact is restricted in the limits which fall to it. The painting has fulness, the poem scope; the one renders much, the other suggests much. Perusing the one, we are students; perusing the other, we are artists. The color gives a limit and a curb to imagination, against which, if not divinely rendered, it will often chafe; the word is a starting-point and stimulus to imagination, to which it only returns as the key and storehouse of its treasures.

The fact, that in poetry the imagination acts directly

on the imagination, through signs in themselves meaningless, — that, in its presentations of spiritual phenomena, it can reach them, aside from their visible forms and effects, sporting between a bold fact and an intangible conception, in the light and out of the light, as suits its necessity or its pleasure, — that it completely renders nothing, but leaves all things to be rendered by the recipient, or rather, the aroused mind, gives it a scope and power which belong to no other art. Add to this, that in metre and music it often has the aid of a new sense which does not elsewhere appear in the arts, and its pre-eminence is evident.

It does not belong to our plan to treat the arts in their rules, or even fully in the particular application of principles which they present, but to mark the object of each art, and the means at its disposal. The mastery of these means is largely mechanical, and falls to the artist alone. Their application to the office or object of the art when known must be within, and subject to, those principles of taste already laid down. The application of these principles in individual cases is practical criticism, — a species of skill to be acquired by familiarity with works of art, and by their careful and protracted study. The application of principles involves a training of the perceptive and judicial powers quite distinct from a mere knowledge of principles. The meter, with all its graduations and possible uses, may be known, but skilful manipulation still remains to be acquired, or it fails of its office.

The first group, gardening and architecture, is that of utility. They indicate the skill and power, and at the same time the pleasure, with which man reaches his physical good. While in these arts perfectly shaping the material at his disposal to a magnificent realization of his wants, he shows leisure to utter feeling, and delight the mind with concurrent beauties.

The second group is primarily representative, and memorative. Sculpture and painting are reproductive of our most noble and most stirring facts, — the reflection of the fullest things in nature and man. They struggle to commemorate the high virtue which time has struck down, the startling beauty which the changing elements have abolished, or the feeling which the yet more shifting tide of thought hastes to snatch away.

These arts are the counterparts of the real, having in them the facts, the truths, the ideals of nature.

The third group, as opposed to the other two, is intellectual, not as addressing the intellect, but as lying solely in the intellect without any external, material creation corresponding to the internal impression. In its inherent power, this group is stimulative and sympathetic, — the medium through which we lend our impulses and our feelings to all.

We shall consider these six arts in their order, commencing with gardening.

In each of these, our only object will be to determine the province of the art, or, more definitely, the aims open to it, and the means by which these are to be reached. A knowledge of the manner in which these means are to be employed does not necessarily belong to one who merely judges the effects and results of art, — who decides upon the æsthetical merit, the beauty of a work. There are two points open for judgment in any work of art; — its actual power and expression; the difficulties met and overcome in reaching this power.

The first pertains to intrinsic merit or value, the second to the skill and ingenuity evinced. The one is a question of taste, which any mind of quick and cultivated perceptions may without assumption answer, the very inquiry being, What is the impression which the work is fitted to make on natures duly sensitive? The other is a question of art, of contrivance and manual skill, only to be rightly answered by those familiar with the methods and difficulties of the work, — by artists.

The first of these points is not to be relinquished to the amateur and artist.

We are not to be told what is beautiful, and assigned the irksome task of admiring it. We are, so far as possessed of a trained and cultivated nature, the judges of art, and that is good art which quickens and gratifies our feelings. He who is able to feel and admire the works of God, *a fortiori* is able to appreciate and admire those of man; and this is the touchstone of these works, — their ability to arouse interest and fill the soul of man. In one respect the artist is even less able to judge correctly a work of art, in its claims to beauty, than one in other respects of equal culture. The two considerations of merit and skill, in themselves so distinct, will inevitably be mingled in his decisions. Much work is admired which has slight claims to intrinsic beauty, simply because the honest opinions and feelings of men are overborne by artistic judgments. Those who are authorized to judge do not dare either to ask themselves what they like, or not to seem to like what artists have imperatively told them they must like.

Opinions, therefore, which in their formation may have much greater reference to ingenuity and clever craft than to simple and powerful expression, which even may have arisen from the prejudices and perversions of artists, often overrule the sentiments of educated communities, and leave them the awkward devotees of a costly art, from which they receive no pleasure, and in which they find no compensation.

All that we can and shall say will have reference to the first point, will tacitly rest upon an assertion of our right to judge the intrinsic beauty of works of art, and, by showing the scope and range of such works, will strive to aid us in rendering a correct judgment.

In all instances, a knowledge of the relations and offices of an object is requisite to judge of the felicity of the method in which these are met. This is true equally in nature and art. We must possess, therefore, the general principles which circumscribe and guide any art, which give form and limit to its products, before we can render a tolerably accurate judgment of its results.

Gardening is primarily a useful art, whose aim is to furnish those vegetables and fruits which support life and gratify taste. In most cases, it but slightly transcends this, its first object; yet, in the regularity of its forms and the accuracy of its lines, good gardening often betrays a secret aspiration for the beautiful. This ambition, however, only becomes obvious and avowed when the utility aimed at is enlarged, and becomes less direct and marketable. A park is said to be the lungs of a city. The garden and surrounding grounds are the lungs of a family, and when men begin to stretch their stakes, lengthen their walks, and expand their culture, that they may enclose for their own immediate use more of earth and air, and give to their leisure hours a healthy ventilation, and to the family a larger out-door life, there will immediately arise a new and stronger demand for beauty, and we shall have landscape gardening, a fine art.

The prime utility here is air and healthy exercise, to which art comes in to add the much higher emotional and intellectual utility of beauty and truth, locked up in living organisms. Physical utility, however, at the very outset, assigns a law severe and imperative to landscape gardening.

The enclosure of the individual for strictly personal pleasures must have limits relatively narrow. The first, last, and abiding impression must not be of the greed and egotism of the owner, as of one who would be alone on the earth, — who devours up, in his luxuries, the vineyard of Naboth, the gardens of the poor, — who possesses more than he can use, and aims at impression through magnitude, — the last resort of selfish, vulgar wealth. This does not, indeed, interfere with great physical beauty in all parts of such lordly grounds; yet this beauty is overpowered and destroyed in its effect by being put to the wretched work of expressing the foolish vanity or heartless pride of the owner. There must be a broad, just, and humane democracy in a man's faith, actions, and possessions, before, in their relations to him, they can be right, they can be beautiful.

The garden is the family portion in God's sunlight, air, and earth, — the breathing-place of our spiritual nature, of gratitude and of love, and as such it should show the affectionate hand of the owner, and be proportioned to his modest wants and rights. No usurpation should find place here, — no second-hand pride, padded with the real and modest virtues of artists and gardeners. The seminary and the college, the village and the city, may have their ample grounds on which wealth lavishes itself, for these represent the combined wants of many, and often what the rich are willing to do for the poor. A grand park in the centre of a crowded and gasping population is man uniting with God to restore the inspired gospel of nature, of pure light and of open heavens, to those crushed and buried under brick and mortar.

The world is not so small, however, but that each may, with modesty, in most localities, take for himself a very considerable portion, and a larger portion, since it may be readily treated in reference both to agriculture and beauty, and, while quickening the taste of its possessor, render its full quota for the nourishment of man. There is in what has been said no denial of the assertion that the intellectual and æsthetical end is intrinsically of greater value than the physical end, but only the implied assertion that the higher end is best reached under the limitation of the lower.

Having determined that the pleasure-garden must express modesty and moderation in its dimensions, and be within the wants and affectionate treatment of the family, and that it must not be sustained as a useless appendage of wealth, only valuable because costly, we return to our inquiry, What, under these conditions, are its objects and resources?

The object of landscape gardening is the most effective presentation of natural objects, primarily those of the vegetable kingdom, and secondarily those of the inorganic. The material belongs to nature: cultivation, calling forth the best powers of herb, shrub, and tree; and arrangement, skilfully combining these into the most pleasing product, belong to man. The world is full of natural beauty altogether aside from man's action upon it; indeed, this beauty more frequently suffers from his passions and pursuits, than is aided by his taste. Yet it is capable of receiving such aid, and many of the choice powers of nature are reserved to reward the skill and affection of man. The world invites the exercise of taste by the new beauties with which she crowns it. This enhanced and condensed effect is the object of landscape gardening, and the problem of the gardener is, How best to secure and present the natural beauties within his reach. Art is here in the service of nature, and hidden under her guise. The garden should show us what contrivance and arrangement have done, or rather have caused nature to do, but not the contrivance and arrangement themselves. This object of gardening gives us at once a very important principle, — that all tricks, deceptions, and palpable conceits are to be laid aside, the artist being everywhere concealed by the luxuriant and native growth of his work. The object is to exhibit living beauties and natural forms, and not human contrivances. This object also will limit the number of architectural works and ornaments that may be employed. In proportion as the garden is rich, various, and full, these should disappear, and only as nature relaxes and becomes more subdued and monotonous may art bring forward her creations. A garden is greatly injured by a self-conceit which tinkers and tutors everything, which cuts and stakes and straightens, till all freedom and scope are fretted away, and nature knows not where to hide herself from her persecutor. The garden does not exhibit the man, but the man's love of lower life, his pleasurable study of one great chapter in the Creator's work.

Having this object definitely before us, — the presentation of natural beauties, — we proceed to inquire what are the resources of the gardener.

(*a.*) First among these are herbs, shrubs, and trees, treated as individual specimens. For this purpose they need to stand alone, that all their lines may be seen, and to receive generous culture, that the native power of the plant may be fully drawn out. Sometimes the plant in its entire, native outline is desired, — the restful and luxuriant ideal of its species. In this case, it is to be sheltered from accident, and from the most awkward of accidents, the pruning-knife. Sometimes one portion of the plant is sacrificed to another, — as in horticulture the boughs to the fruit, and in many shrubs and vines the shoots to the flowers. It is worthy, however, of our notice, that the tree and the nobler and statelier shrubs rely far more on free, symmetrical, and native forms than on flowers for their power, and hold themselves aloof from the curbing and cropping that fall so plentifully on minor plants. The integrity of a plant should, as far as possible, be respected.

(*b.*) A second resource is herbs, shrubs, and trees, grouped in the plot and the plantation. Plants are social, and when clustered mutually modify each other, and often secure a new and striking effect. As herbs are primarily cultivated for the flower, of which color is a prominent element, this as well as form becomes an important consideration in blending them with each other. In a group, resemblance rather than contrast should be sought, as the mind is both more instructed and interested in observing resemblances than in noting differences, and finds more pleasure in the harmony than in the conflict, or even contrast, of color.

Shrubs and trees gathered into clumps lose their independent form, unite in a common life, and present a compound outline with shifting shadows, deep recesses, and variegated surfaces, and thus become possessed of an associated power quite beyond that of the individual.

The grouping of flowers in plots in reference to color and characteristics, and of trees in plantations in reference to outline and power, is an elementary and most important combination in gardening. The ground plan or outline of the plantation will rarely be defined or regular, but the clump will concentrate or expand itself according to the office it has to perform. The outline of the flower-plot, on the other hand, must, from the necessities of cultivation, be distinctly marked. The most easy, and at the same time the most barren, boundaries for these are mathematical figures. The first action of thought always tends to throw this extreme regularity into its products; the growth of feeling soon breaks it up. Complex mathematical and regular forms are less fortunate than these forms when simple. They are too artificial, perplex the eye, and require too much care to maintain them. The best outlines for the plot are secured by plain, easy, and open curves, now uniting in regular, now in irregular yet definite figures, and ever seeming to give free action to the enclosed life, by yielding an open space to its slightest pressure. Outlines of this sort are strokes of fancy whose principal virtue is graceful curvature.

(*c.*) A third resource is the natural advantages which the enclosed ground presents. These are chiefly inequalities and roll of surface, water, and rocks. If these are present in any good degree, they at once give plan and character to the whole work. They afford a harvest of obvious opportunities which the artist carefully gathers, making each striking object a distinct feature, and the central subject of a distinct treatment. The bold variety which nature has so kindly furnished he makes haste to present, clothing the rugged places with their own forms of life, and the richer intervals with the luxurious plants of affluence; suffering the dark evergreen to gather in sad recesses, and the deciduous trees to wander out in free spaces and open sunshine; rejoicing in the rock which bears a stubborn, naked front, and will not away, and in the rivulet which is ever going, yet tarries when the rock is worn to dust.

Among these natural resources, none has been a more general and just favorite than water, especially when presenting a broad surface. Water itself is a strangely subtile element, and, in that inner world of shadows and reflection which such a sheet presents, we have a strong appeal to the imagination, — a silent and magical echo of the fitful world above, itself more fitful still. This recording consciousness of water, who has not loved to watch?

A level field lays a heavier duty on the artist and justifies more of architectural embellishment. An effort to supply the place of natural advantages by artificial excavations and mounds is at best but partially successful, and only possible in connection with those large expenditures which can only accompany public works. Slight mounds are for the most part worthless, arid, and insignificant imitations. This is not true, in the same degree, of water-basins, as these, though small, subserve an obvious purpose, and are not mere faint mimicry of nature. When the ground enclosed presents any distinctive features, the improvement and separate treatment of these give a second principle of combination, and the plot and the plantation are so used as to preserve the individuality and character of these more favored portions.

(*d.*) The fourth element subject to the skill of the gardener are the prospects without the enclosure. These may be both favorable and unfavorable, and he is then desirous to preserve entire the one, and protect himself against the other. Both of these ends are reached through the arrangement of trees and shrubbery. Plantations shelter the eye from the offence of surrounding objects, and substitute for the outbuildings of a neighbor their own green depths and endless diversity. These also, opening out into shady vistas or breaking away into free and airy spaces, leave the eye at liberty to reach a distant beauty or sweep in an adjoining landscape. Surrounding objects give a law to the plan of the garden, a second principle of combination to the foliage. Certain things are to be concealed, certain as carefully retained, and the surroundings, sifted of their deformities, are to come in as most important adjuncts, giving wealth and extension to the garden, and putting it in sympathy with the broad world about it. If views are to be retained, they cannot be equally retained from all points. This would demand an open field and exclude gardening. There must, therefore, be favored points, — out-looks for which these advantages are reserved. The selection and management of these become an early and important question. If the surrounding views are diverse, — some of cities and villages, some of forests and mountains in silent repose, — the question arises, at what points, and upon what conditions, shall this outside world be admitted. Shall the garish light of gleaming walls and glittering spires be made to traverse the long vista, to leap the foliage from bough to bough, till, filtered of the sounds and busy vanity of man, it comes to the silent shrine of the spirit, the washed pilgrim of the distant world? Or shall we roll back our green curtains, and open wide our eager portals that the world in dusty garments, with cart and carriage may drive pell-mell upon us? And that broad sweep of hill and forest, where God works in repose, and is busy in silence, shall we not open our hearts full upon it, and ask it to speak to us from its throne of life, — life, God-given, God-sustained, the divinest thing of earth?

(*e.*) Another distinct and most important element are intervening and open spaces, both in what they give below and above. A taste just aroused will substitute, without compunction, flowers in continuous beds for the smoothest lawn, and the richest carpet ever woven in loom. A little later, and we break the surface with caution and reluctance, gathering the flowers into detached plots, where they may overshadow the soil, and, creeping down to their well-defined border, become the rarer jewels of the green enamel. Open spaces in clear light, and with cautious ornament, give full respiration and cheerful rest to the mind and eye. Nor are they less advantageous in opening up the sky in its azure, than the earth in its green. These two colors, the staples of the upper and the lower fields, have a constant, an hourly mission, and we must not be deficient in these necessities of life. Every good gardener will be cautious how he shears into fragments and patch-work his simplest, and, for that reason, his best and most reliable material.

The lawn also furnishes, in connection with surrounding and scattered objects, an opportunity to avail ourselves of shadows, — the cheerful, evanishing retinue of morning, the spectral thronging crowd of evening. These lovely adjuncts of the coming and departing day, dials of the passing hour, are not to be forgotten. To these open spaces will also belong the encompassing glories which often attend the sunrise and sunset. When the whole arch is a canvas, radiant with Divine workmanship, we would not be smothered in a forest, but lifted out on the naked earth, — the more naked the better, for we now look heavenward.

(*f.*) An important resource of gardening reserved to this point are walks and avenues, — in private grounds, the first being more prominent; in public grounds, the second. Walks are the skeleton of the garden, and largely express, though they do not constitute, its plan. If any of the resources already mentioned furnish distinct points, and give character to any portion of the enclosure, this fact must first be known, and the paths be made to recognize it and conform to it. The land is first to be looked over in reference to its suggestions and possibilities within and without; and these being secured, the outline of paths which include and reach them will begin to be seen. That is a very barren ground in which walks of pleasant curvature and convenient spaces may be placed at random. While the character of the enclosure and the relation of objects will do much to determine the walks, there are other points of interest in their treatment.

(*a.*) Their centre is the dwelling, and to this is their chief relation. As they approach it, they become more direct, as if seized with a definite object.

(*b.*) They are to be managed with a constant recollection of the fact that they are paths to be walked in, and that men love, even in rambling, to have an object, to go somewhere, and also, that in reaching such an object, they do not unnecessarily make sharp curves, or pursue a circuitous, wasting, zigzag path, but, unless prevented by some obstacle, approach directly, with only minor fluctuations. This directness is not often to lapse into a straight line, for such a line is less pleasing than a curve, reveals at the outset all the ground to be passed over, and belongs to the theodolite, and not to nature. On the other hand, if a large circuit is obviously made, a reason must be rendered for it in the presence of an intervening obstruction. Paths, for they are paths of men, are not to wander purposeless and wild over a field, as if they had gone mad.

(*c.*) Walks should be few. Their gravelly surfaces are barren to the eye, they are kept with much labor, and are, after all, a constraint. We feel as strangers when everywhere told by these trim monitors to keep off the grass. The object of a garden is not to walk forever on gravel, but to get off the gravel. Where the travel is not so direct or constant as to destroy the sod, let your foot fall silently on the fresh, living lap of earth, God's gift to your sandal.

(*d.*) Walks are, as far as possible, to take the place of avenues. In a large park accessible to many only in carriages, and essentially a public place, these broad belts of gravel, where affluence rolls leisurely along, ostensibly to admire nature, in fact itself to be admired, are unavoidable. But I know not why they should be admitted further than necessity requires. A garden is not to be driven through on a trot, or looked over on horseback. It is a volume to be quietly, slowly read, and communed with. He who visits his garden in a carriage, has no garden, and cheats himself and his friends with a fantasy.

(*g.*) Last among the resources, or at least the adjuncts, of gardening may be placed the enclosing hedges, walls, or fences, and architectural ornaments. An enclosure is a necessity, rather than a beauty. The presumption is against a fence; it must always show reason for its presence. It is rather characteristic of American taste to delight in fences. This may in part arise from the fact that it has been the first duty of the emigrant to fence in his own from the unfenced wilderness, and that a sense of work done, of ownership secured, does not arise till a good rail zigzag, fretted with stakes, marks his borders. However this may be, the farmer who owns hundreds of acres insists upon one, two, or three narrow enclosures about his dwelling, and the village resident must show his wealth in a costly and obtrusive fence, necessarily destitute of architectural value, and with its glare of paint striving to atone to the eye for the verdure which should be behind it.

Where fences must be, they should be as simple and unobtrusive as possible, being in themselves unworthy of any great expense, and little fitted for ornament by their rough service. A high, heavy fence gives the impression, on the outside, of cool reserve, of an army in trenches, and on the inside of constraint. It must have its origin in necessity. Seclusion can be reached through trees without thrusting a blank wall in the face of the innocent traveller. It is a sad comment on public virtue when every picket seems designed to impale a thief, and one looks for grim-visaged death on a garden fence as on castle pikes. Nature offers us retirement, robbed of its sour pride and saucy impudence, in the living hedge; yet even this will be used with caution, if we are willing to refresh the passer-by with what God has granted for our refreshment, if we are willing to add this, our private beauty, to the beauty of the world. It is also to be remembered that he who fences out the eye of a stranger, by a gracious retribution, fences himself in, robs his grounds of that catholic sympathy in which nature loves to stand with herself.

Gardening stands in close relation to architecture, being usually the dependant of the dwelling. Architecture, with its bridges, trellises, arbors, and conservatories, may furnish gardening fine embellishments; but in proportion as the garden is itself affluent, these are not required, and, if present, should be of a rural character. Elaborate and careful architecture is better near the dwelling and subservient to it, than when striving with natural beauties for attention. With yet more propriety does the dwelling keep at a distance all larger shrubs and trees, suffering nothing to tower just at hand in contrast with it, chafing it, or concealing it. If it has any architectural merit, this should meet and satisfy the eye. Vines, and the more dependent and modest shrubs, seeking support and shelter, join themselves to the dwelling, while the rank, independent, and stately growths retreat a little, as not venturing to crowd upon their principal. Protection and shelter are indeed desirable in the vicinity of the house, but not less are air and sunlight. This union of the residence with its surroundings, through lesser and unobtrusive plants, will best meet the conditions of use, will preserve the integrity of architecture and gardening as independent sources of expression, and also mark their sympathy with each other.

In the primary end of gardening — a presentation of natural beauties fitted to elicit and interest the feelings, — there are included many subsidiary ends. It is sufficient to mention a few of these, — shelter and seclusion ; variety, reached by a careful separation and distinction of members in the garden, not suffering the eye to range beyond the department immediately before it ; unity, the mutual connection of these portions, by which each unites to complete without repeating the other ; contrast and harmony.

The principal æsthetical powers called forth and cultivated in the artist by landscape gardening are (*a*) perception, (*b*) combination, (*c*) conception.

Too much stress can hardly be laid upon the familiar study of natural objects, as refining and correcting the taste, and enabling the student, with much knowledge of elementary forms and with a correct standard of excellence, to pass to the other arts. All art should be rooted in a careful and loving estimate of the workmanship of the world. He who has not been trained to an appreciative love of nature, will be a poor worker and guide in art.

The artist is also, in a manner, creative. He uses the material at his disposal, but he unites it into a new and powerful effect. This effect is the product of his arranging and combining power, — of his treatment, and exhibits that use and mastery of resources which is the only creation open to human genius.

In conceiving this effect, in reaching this predetermined result, the imagination is disciplined. The results of an act, as of planting or felling a tree, are sometimes remote, sometimes not easily corrected; and to make each step successful, the mind needs to have these consequences in distinct anticipation, to see clearly both the thing to be reached and the steps by which it is reached. The imagination, with many and most complex particulars, accompanies the intuitive, creative reason, and goes before the executive hand; brings the conception to its birth in the mind, and to its later birth in the world of facts.

Italian gardening, chiefly prevalent on the Continent, is much more constrained and artificial than English gardening. It is pleased with mathematical lines, figures, and spaces; uses the shears constantly; unites its flowers in so complicated a plan as to require a bird's-eye view for its comprehension; and is excessively fond of statuary and objects of art. The English park or garden is much more free and simple in its method; devotes itself to fine lawn, magnificent foliage, and trees of famous growth. An occasional avenue of old oaks or elms reaches sublimity; while the cheerfully-sunny glades, and the open spaces which command the front of the dwelling, put upon the landscape a warm and bright face, a cheerful invitation to Heaven's gifts.

LECTURE XII.

ARCHITECTURE.—ITS OBJECTS.—AS A FINE ART.—OFFICES. — SKILL. — ORNAMENT. — RESOURCES OF THE ARCHITECT.— MATERIALS.—MEMBERS: WALL, APERTURES, ROOF, PITCH, DOME.

IN passing to architecture, we come yet more immediately under the law of utility. Use, and more frequently a plain, palpable, physical use, gives rise to the architectural product. Men do not build — do not wearily chisel the stone, mix the mortar, and carry the hod — without a most distinct and recognizable end. They may, indeed, strive to do their work well, to do it beautifully, but this beauty is only the manner in which, and not the end for which, they do it. Beauty does not assign ends, but only methods and means in architecture. Men do not say, I will build beauty, but I will build a beautiful dwelling, a beautiful church. In the words dwelling and church are contained the purpose of the work, in the adjective beautiful the manner of its execution. This purpose must furnish a direction and end to action before any opportunity, any material, is given in whose handling beauty may show her power. The sculptor must have his design before he can carve; the architect must have his task before he can realize a significant execution.

It is plain that means can never rightly interfere with ends, that all such interference betrays a want of power in the worker, an unconquered obstinacy and inflexibility in the material, baffling the architect. Means that retard, thwart, or modify an end cease to be means, and by so much cut us off from our purposes. The same is true of the method, the manner, in which an end is reached, and of the concomitants of that end. These are each subsidiary to the end itself. If we are correct, therefore, in affirming that beauty is a method, a manner, a concomitant, it thence follows that it does not govern the end, but is itself governed by that end; that utility in architecture assigns a law to beauty from which it may not depart; and that any such departure, any, the slightest, conflict of ornament with use destroys beauty. The beauty is not the utility, but the significant, the thoughtful and emotional manner in which that utility is reached. This relation of utility and beauty must be distinctly apprehended for the right understanding of architecture. We shall then be no longer misled by detached members, isolated beauties, by portions in themselves correct, but shall judge the whole as a whole, in its relation to its great purpose, and in its relation to each of its constituents. In good architecture, a single end will be seen, sending forth its mandate everywhere, and everywhere securing a cheerful and perfect obedience.

Architecture, as a fine art, has reference to man's work, and is dependent for its power on the success, the excellency of that work; first, as exhibiting thought, an accurate, vigorous, and grand adaptation of means to an end; second, as exhibiting feeling, — the pleasure with which the mind treats the forms and surfaces of its work, striving to make them expressive of its own emotions. Architecture exhibits the intellectual and emotional resources of man, and this is its beauty, its object as a fine art, and it can only exist as a fine art, as and because it is a useful art. The breadth and success of its use are the framework of its beauty. In gardening, man presents the work of God, living products, perfectly and highly wrought; in architecture, he presents his own work, his power over material in itself now more, now less admirable. In the one case, the object is prominent; in the other, its treatment. In the one product, we see how God works; in the other, how man works with that which God gives him. The scope of architecture in the realm of beauty is the intellectual and emotional power which it expresses as the work of man.

The utilities which architecture seeks are various, falling with moderate accuracy into three classes.

Its earliest and most constant end is protection. Buildings for protection constitute the first and larger class of edifices. Unsheltered man has sought shelter; and shelter with man includes the gratification of many wants, the protection and nurture of a group of numerous instincts, affections, and tastes. The dwelling is the orb of childhood, the nest, the nursery, and school of the human callow: it is the home of manhood, its centre of exertion and enjoyment, its points of departure and return: it is the repose of age; thither, weary and spent, it turns to lay down its burden. Such a retreat, lasting and manifold in its offices, will gradually build into itself, will come slowly to contain, all fortunate contrivances, fine adaptations, and strokes of feeling, — the grand, the simple and the emotional conceptions of man. As the shell of the snail and the shield of the turtle yield to the included life, — shape themselves with curious skill and kind provision to all its necessities, so the home of man in its forms bespeaks the wants and wisdom of its inmate, the ends and means of the human worker, and records in bark hut or solid masonry the growth and convolutions of rational life.

Architecture commences with the dwelling. This is the first labor that the necessities of shelter assign to man. There immediately follow in the interests of commerce other forms of protective edifices, — the shop, store, factory, warehouse, custom-house, bank, and exchange; in the interests of education, the school-house, academy, seminary, college, observatory, library, public hall; in those of government, the prison, fort, court-house, legislative hall; and in those of religion, the church, cathedral, temple. This department of protective architecture is most various and inclusive, — from the house of the hermit, to the hall that springs its vaulted roof above the heads of thousands; from the thin thatch that turns the pattering rain, to the solid stone and stern battlements that stand amid the hail of iron; from the coy arbor flecking the sunshine, to the defiant light-house, sentinel of the night-ocean, baffling the malignant waves with a single, persistent truth.

The second end of architecture, giving rise to another class of structures, is transit. To this class belong bridges, aqueducts, and tunnels. The object here is to give passage, sometimes through, sometimes over, an obstacle. The direct effect of the masonry is support, — the path lying on it or passing under it; in the one case, the burden being that of the footman, the vehicle, the transmitted water; in the other, the incumbent earth or buildings.

A third, a monumental class of structures, are the memorials of the dead and of historic events. Here, the object is an affectionate remembrance of kindred and friends, or a patriotic remembrance of national events and heroes.

In each of these classes, the character and outline of the work are determined by its office, and precisely as this office is complete and explicit in its demands will it control all the details of form. The dwelling fulfils a most complex end, the monument a simple end. The form of the first is therefore more perfectly subjected to the law of use than that of the second, and the second left more open than the first to the action of feeling.

Architecture becomes a fine art, addresses itself to the tastes and feelings of men, through the thoughtful and emotional manner in which the particular objects of protection, transit, or monition are reached. The beauty, then, of an architectural work is dependent on two particulars: the thought and the feeling evinced, its form as resulting from a duty faithfully and felicitously fulfilled, its form and surfaces as subsidiarily affected by feeling. The first is skill, mastery of means; the second, ornament.

All the grander, stronger impressions of architecture are due to the first, the admirable obedience of matter to mind, the powerful working of thought, successful execution following in the steps of bold conception, with a clear reconciliation of members and concurrence of offices in one leading object. Without these, ornament becomes trivial and nugatory. In this respect, the beauty of the work depends on the power and precision of the thought. By its power in the pursuit of any end, it hits on the right relation, combination, or form; by its precision, it cuts away all that overlies and conceals its conception, and reveals this right combination or form in clear outline. It equally rejects too much and too little, and is only satisfied when its entire thought is made visible in distinct contour. Power is seen in the arch, and precision in the care with which it is cut to, without infringing on, the curve of pressure, thus revealing the line of force. So, too, the capital, column, and base are wrought to their office, and have every exigency of their office chiseled into the lines of their form. The swell, the bevel, the taper speak of the adding of needful, or the cutting away of superfluous material. For the full apprehension of this class of beauties in architecture, we must know the duty of each member in the variety of its offices. Thus only shall we see the perfection of the form in which these are expressed and met.

The secondary element through which architecture becomes a fine art is ornament. A large number of subsidiary beauties are due to this. The leading end does not so definitively rule surfaces or the details of form, as not to suffer feeling, within certain limits, to work upon these, and redeem them from a blankness and poverty into which they would otherwise fall. Unoccupied ground, for which neither thought, nor feeling have done anything, unaffected by the exigencies of the work or the fancy of the worker, is unpleasant. Ornament enters in to occupy the spaces as yet unoccupied of art, to shape and modify form within the limits of use. Ornament is not for this reason extraneous or foreign to the building. It twines itself into and beautifies the framework of the edifice, as a vine clings to an arbor-lattice, and is true ornament only as it perfects the original design. Sometimes the primary end will include more, sometimes less, of this its rich and graceful accompaniment, and true, chaste ornamentation will ever feel and respect the limits thus assigned it.

Before proceeding to speak further of the classes of architecture, we need to understand the resources of the architect.

His standard materials are three, — stone, brick, wood, — to which, for a variety of purposes, a fourth is now added. These materials are by no means equally abundant or good in all localities. Especially are the best quarries limited in their range. Stone which is of a uniform texture, firm, yet of easy cleavage, pleasing in color and capable of being secured in large blocks, is comparatively rare, and when present must always exert a powerful influence on architecture. Edifices like those of Greece, with massive lintels, majestic and smooth-chiseled columns, could not exist in less favored regions. Adjacent rocks, whether gray granite, brown sandstone, blue limestone, or marble, will at once give character to the architecture of a city or province. The more influential considerations in the stone at the disposal of the artist are size, hardness, and color. Stone which exists only in fragments, which is too flaky to be quarried in solid blocks, precludes some of the more imposing and perfect features of architecture. The face and columns of an edifice of such material must present the roughness of rubble compost, instead of a firm, homogeneous, and carefully wrought surface. Small stones are inconsistent with symmetry and lightness of form, sharp outline and ornamental carving, and will sometimes demand a surface coat of mortar by which the true character of the building is lost. A very hard stone discourages the chisel, and lies less firmly in the wall; a very soft stone fails to retain the labor expended upon it, and both renders, and seems to render, the edifice insecure. A degree of hardness which leaves the stone susceptible to the workman's thought, and, at the same time retentive of it, must ever be influential on the character of the work, especially on its ornament.

In the colors of stone there is certainly a choice, but more important in color than original shade are uniformity and durability. Stones of a mixed character and changeable color greatly detract from the effect. In some climates at least the purest marble seems less appropriate than granite or sandstone for out-door work, as too little suited to escape the soil and stain of the elements. The sober gray of solid granite is well fitted for the harsh seaboard of New England. Upon this original character and the particular office of the stone will depend the propriety of a rough or smooth finish. The coarse-grained stones, made to face the storms, are often left to advantage in their fresh native cleavage, the chiseled edges alone marking the attention and care of the workman. There are a certain boldness and rapidity of workmanship in these rough Titan blocks, a distinguishing between what is necessary and what may be dispensed with, that often render the effect most pleasing. Stones from their texture capable of a perfect polish, or somewhat more sheltered in the position assigned them, or bearing ornament, demand a careful finish.

Brick, as a material of the artist, is greatly inferior to stone, entirely precludes carving, requires a cornice and column wholly its own, and, though not incapable of reaching considerable excellence, must ever be entirely inadequate for the best work.

Small buildings suffer less than large buildings from this material. The dwelling with no broad surfaces and with considerable variety of outline, may employ it to advantage. It deserves to be questioned, whether the prevalent method of pencilling, by which each brick is carefully distinguished, is not a vicious treatment drawing attention to the tale of brick rather than overcoming their inherent difficulty, their too great divisibility, and uniting them in a uniform surface.

The fact, that paint both for mechanical and æsthetical reasons is rightly applied to brick, testifies to their inherent weakness.

Wood, as the framework and outside of a building, has as advantages, the facility with which it receives form, and renders a smooth surface, and usually its cheapness; as disadvantages, its deficiency in strength, durability, and for some climates at least, in protection.

These defects are less serious in small buildings than in large, and, while wood can never dispute the field with stone in any important work, it may often displace brick in dwellings and more transient structures. Wood in outside work requires paint, but certainly not that white paint which, in full light, is to the eye the most painful and glaring of colors, and finds no sympathy in nature, unless it be in the chaste shroud of the buried year, in winter, the tomb of living beauty.

In cities, iron begins to occupy ground once possessed by brick and stone, with this loss, that it makes the most elaborate architecture relatively cheap and contemptible. Capitals and cornice, cast by a pattern, ceasing to have the feeling, will cease to have the value which attaches to the product of the chisel. There must be a certain amount of personality back of even the best work to sustain its value. Flowers which exactly repeated each other would lose our sympathy. Buildings succeeding each other in mechanical exactness of imitation divide and subdivide, and finally destroy, our interest. A hundred thousand engravings cannot each have at their disposal the power of the first painting, but only some remote fraction of it. Every impression which falls from the plate places us one remove further from the centre of interest and art, the mind of the worker. This principle must and will be regarded in architecture. That which is wrought in stone with freedom and freshness of thought will strive in pattern and outline to distinguish itself from, and to assert its superiority over, the now vulgar herd of ornaments which have but one thought for a thousand, and multiply themselves with less care and variety than pebbles on a beach.

When we pass to the material of inside architecture, the variety is greater, though the pre-eminence still remains with wood and stone, this difference only being marked, that wood has now more extensive, numerous, and striking adaptations than stone. The many varieties of wood present themselves in the native beauty of their internal structure in all richer work, no longer requiring the protection or suffering the disguise of paints. The lightness, toughness, elasticity, and warmth of wood, the ease with which it is worked, and the beauty of its veining, give it for many purpose a fitness, a natural superiority over the colder and less tractable marbles and metals. Elaborate work in ivory and the precious metals owes the esteem in which it is held quite as much to superior cost as to superior beauty. In the less costly, though not the less dear and influential, architecture of the home, paints, papers, and plaster must find admission as the cheap pliant materials of taste, and from an honest yet skilful handling may receive no small share of value.

The final constituents of the building are the materials now spoken of; but there is also a subdivision of the building itself into certain parts or members, which are to be treated separately, and which present distinct problems to the architect. The more distinct and important of these demand separate mention.

First is the wall. This has several members, the broad foot or base partly hidden in the soil by which it connects itself with, and firmly rests upon, the ground; the vail, or wall proper, which, reduced in thickness, rests on this base; and the cornice or top of the wall which, with its broad surface, receives and evenly diffuses the weight of the roof, and with its projecting mouldings sheds the water. The base and the cornice, the one in its nearness, the other in its projection, present prominent features for outline and ornament. The wall is usually sought both for shelter and support; it may have the latter office only. In that case, the wall-vail is rolled as it were into a series of columns, their capitals and bases even more distinct and carefully treated than in the wall.

With no especial philosophy or correctness, earlier architecture, more especially Grecian architecture, has been divided by the character of the capital which these columns have received. The capitals are not so distinct or so controlling features of modern architecture as to claim the position assigned them in this classification. The wall-vail perpetually tends to blank surfaces. These, aside from ornament, are broken in several ways. The building may divide itself into stories,—into distinct strata by a band of new and more firm material. This will most readily occur in a building of brick by the insertion of a layer of broad, uniform stone. The wall may strengthen itself by half-merged columns or pilasters, and thus reach the required end with an economy of material and change of surface. The wall may support itself against the lateral thrust of the roof by a tower or by a buttress. But that which more than anything else relieves the wall are the apertures for the admission of persons and of light. The door-way is a leading feature in any building. With its deep and broad recess, open jambs, arch-head, and folding leaves, the favorite seat of ornament; or with its single leaf and straight contour, it is at once sought by the eye. The greater the surface of wall, the larger, more imposing and beautiful should be the entrance, from the increased dignity of its office, from the relief it furnishes the eye, and from the interpretation which it gives to the mind of the purpose of the edifice. Ordinary entrances to great buildings at once reduce them in character.

As far as size is concerned, the same is true, in a somewhat less degree, of apertures for the admission of light. These, as more numerous and secondary in office, though less important members of the building than the door-ways, are yet the principal feature of the side walls, and thus require the chief attention. They are liable to lose their value from barrenness of form, and monotonous repetition. A wall-vail with square apertures at fixed intervals is scarcely less blank than when unpierced. These disadvantages are often needlessly incurred, often directly sought after. The square, plain lintel is preferred to the carved and arched lintel, an irregular or triangular space is occupied by a square aperture, small windows are inserted at short intervals, without reference to use, and even against use, as if the first axiom of architecture were the greatest number of windows in the most regular ranks, with the least in each of individual value. Windows that stand in precisely the same relations cannot, indeed, be readily varied in form, but the value of each should be made as great as possible, their number reduced, and, with each change of relation, as in passing from story to story, or from a broad surface to one restricted in extent, or irregular in outline, the contour should be varied. Correct taste will quickly show its growth in the treatment of windows, thrusting aside the much sought after uniformity, and giving to each window or rank of windows its own duty and character. They can only thus become interesting features, relieving the wall of which they form a part.

In the wall, as adjuncts, are included the base, the cornice, the capital, the column, the band, the pilaster, the buttress, the turret, the door, and the window, with their arch-heads, jambs, and lintels.

The second leading member of the edifice is the roof. Though quite separable in office, and usually in form, we shall treat under this term the covering of the passage-way and of the enclosure. The passage-way is roofed for support, the enclosure for shelter.

The space-way of the door and of the window must

be spanned, in order that the wall may proceed above it. The piers of the bridge must be united, that the stream may find passage beneath, and the travel flow on above, the two currents interwoven, but unobstructed. The tunnel arched in the loose soil gives transit without removing the obstacle. In these and similar cases, the passage-way may be regarded as an aperture in a a wall of greater or less thickness, and the question to be, How shall the strength of the wall be maintained, the portions above finding adequate support? The most simple method, as in the door-way or the culvert, is to pass a timber or a flat stone of adequate dimensions from side to side. The cornices of the Greek porches and colonnades were so supported, resting on the capitals, and sustained in the intervals by the tenacity of the material. This method, though simple, has in all work of brick and stone, where the weight is great, most serious difficulties. It demands the most favorable material, taxes the strength of that material to the utmost, is unable safely to span a broad passage, and substitutes a barren straight line for the most pleasing curves.

The arch, once discovered, by its superior aptness largely displaced the flat lintel where either strength or beauty was desired. It is only minor passage-ways, bearing no great burden, in which this weak and barren form is oftenest used. To the windows and door-ways of wooden edifices, the consideration of strength real or apparent does not apply, but only that of beauty. There will be freedom and variety in the curve of the arch in proportion as the pressure relaxes. As this increases, the arch will bow itself to the burden, and approximate the curve of greatest strength. The wise artist will strive not to conceal, but to reveal in the contour of the included aperture the character of the duty which the arch is performing, cutting close to the curve of pressure when this is stringent and severe. The arch is frequently limited in the height to which it may rise. It may strike, as over the window, into a high and sharp point, or, as in spanning the river, it may be compelled to lie low and broad in a flat arc, dipping in its transit like an aquatic bird close to the water. The number of the offices which the arch can perform, and the ease and variety of the methods in which it meets them all, impart to it great beauty. The forms which it assumes are thoroughly thoughtful, and may well, therefore, be beautiful.

It is the generic office of an arch to bear a burden. It is this very burden which consolidates and strengthens it, and enables the piers and abutments to endure its side thrust. It is not for this reason so well fitted for mere shelter. The high thin walls which sustain the roof of a building must, as far as possible, be relieved from all lateral pressure, and an arch resting upon these without strong and low girders would result in their immediate overthrow. The roofs of enclosures therefore are often so constructed as to reduce all pressure to vertical lines, to the support of their own weight. This is more especially necessary in large buildings, — in buildings of stone and brick where the opposing walls are less perfectly girded to each other. Flat roofs supported by the walls and included partitions have no architectural interest, and will only exist in cities, where the roof of the dwelling is unseen; in countries where the roof is the resort of the inmates; and in buildings in one feature at least without architectural claims. In most buildings which stand independent, the roof not only diverts the storms, but incloses a valuable space, — is not a mere floor laid flatly on to cover an open top, but an expressive and completing member of manifold offices. These roofs in their most simple forms are composed of two planes — in their more complex forms they contain no new principle — inclined against each other, which by action in exactly opposite directions, neutralize each in each, through interior connections, every other pressure but that of weight, and rest as one integral burden on the side walls, or on those interior supports which the purposes of the building may suffer it to render. Such roofs present, without, broad surfaces and high gables, and within, the deep recesses of nave and transept. These vaulted ceilings — in the large spaces they give, in the grand, airy way in which they perform their office, in the suggestions which they furnish in their complicated lines and interlacing timbers of mechanical skill and power, and in the many points which they present for ornament — are favorite and noble features in architecture.

In the expression of a roof, its pitch, the eaves, the tile, the balustrade, and chimneys, are the salient points. A steep pitch is connected with a severe and rugged climate, both historically and through its greater ability to shed the snow and hail of a bleak region. The sharp angles of such a structure give it a more bold and defiant appearance, and the resulting extent of roof surface perpetually reminds one of the important office this member discharges. A flat roof, on the other hand, lies more concealed, sinking with the mildness of the climate into a secondary office and from under vision.

Entirely in harmony with this, the low roof frequently receives a balustrade whose vertical surface conceals it, and presents a more pleasing object than a plane lying so nearly edgewise to the eye. The steep roof, on the other hand, takes various colored, ornamental, diamond, or crested tile, and then ventures to lift itself, an unbroken plane to the eye, or with here and there a gable. The chimney also becomes a more conspicuous and hence more important object in the steep than in the flat roof. Projecting eaves, though not necessarily confined to either style of roof, are more frequently associated with the sharp angle. Such eaves then leave at the top of the wall deep, sheltered, and shady, recesses, dispensing with cornice and removing ornament to the roof-edge, and in the gables to the verge-board. The flat roof with projecting eaves opens up these recesses, and prepares the way for showy brackets. A broad, heavy, Grecian cornice demands a large building with a flat roof and slight projection. The massive stone-work of our larger public edifices prepares the way for this form of covering.

The dome, akin in effect to the vaulted roof, is also nearly allied to the arch. A section of the arch revolved around the crown-point gives the dome. In the dome, the height of the arch, the smallness of the burden, and strength of material, reduce the lateral thrust, and no work in architecture expresses greater airiness, lightness, and facility of position. The roof includes among its adjuncts, the balustrade, gable, spire, and dome.

LECTURE XIII.

ARCHITECTURE. — PROTECTIVE ARCHITECTURE: DWELLING, FARM-HOUSE, COTTAGE, VILLA, CHURCHES. — CHARACTER. — PUBLIC BUILDINGS.

HAVING seen both the material at the disposal of the architcct, and the prominent members into which this is first combined, we may better understand some of the leading æsthetical ends to be reached in the several classes of architecture. These are incidental to a complete fulfilment of the purpose, with its numerous specifications, for which the building is, or should be erected. In protective architecture, we shall only refer to three of its more important kinds of structure, dwellings, churches, and public buildings.

Dwellings, though not giving opportunity for the highest architecture, are, nevertheless, through their greater number and their immediate connection with the daily wants and feelings of all men, a most interesting class of structures. The taste of a people is more indicated and trained by these than by any other buildings. As the dwelling expresses and fulfils the wants of a single family, good taste here precludes arrogance and parade, on the principle before presented in landscape gardening. The real wants of the family are in themselves limited. Too much has in it something of the same embarrassment as too little. Extravagant dimensions and elaborate ornament bespeak an expenditure utterly uncalled for by the end to be reached; worse than this, in a world yet full of hovels, it speaks of an eager, selfish gluttony of enjoyments, a willingness to waste on cumbersome and awkward luxuries the wealth plucked from a famishing world; it stands in flat contradiction to the true democratic spirit and equality of men. The Christian citizen sinks into a cunning and ravenous though tasteful creature gathering into his own lair the most possible of prey. The building which represents character, moral purpose, and principle, the beautiful building, will always show a tacit submission of private pleasures to the public good, — a modest appreciation of one's self when weighed with a world. A baronial mansion implies superior rights, deep-seated hereditary inequalities. The mind that really believes in, and delights in man, will find slight compensation for the beauty which should attach itself to every home, in the magnificent residence of some lordling. That which rightly belongs to industry and intelligence is essentially the same for all. The dwelling which shows the lavish prodigality of fortune toward a favorite teaches the immorality of chance government and of irresponsible expenditure. The dwelling which shows what skill and taste can do with ordinary resources exhibits the beneficence of God, and the grateful appreciation of man, and, no longer the despair of poverty, becomes to all the stimulus of hopeful exertion.

The style of good domestic architecture will naturally distinguish itself from that of public buildings in the material employed, the size and adaptations of the edifice, and in the expenditure for which it provides. Obvious as is this principle, it has been largely overlooked in this country, and one of the most inappropriate of styles for domestic purposes has been more frequently than any other employed in our dwellings.

A heavy Grecian cornice is habitual with us, and massive Grecian columns not unfrequent. The largest marble temples find their absurd imitation in the pine dwelling, a most complete and unthinking oversight of the expression and proprieties of the Grecian style.

Domestic architecture admits of much variety, but in all forms — its bracketted and Gothic, northern and southern — it should recognize the quiet simplicity of its purpose, the lightness and cheapness of its material, and be cautious of borrowing from more dignified and imposing buildings.

The first exertion of taste results in uniformity, — the careful repetition of single forms, through a rectangular building, — this barren order the mind first opposes to disorder. This result is strictly incipient; the taste at once wearies of it, and substitutes regularity, — a careful correspondence of opposite members. This it may take with it into many of its noblest works. Regularity, by which the building can be divided into two halves, each the counterpart of the other, may admit great variety, and, in the larger edifices, where the number of members is in itself great, may serve to give a noble unity and power to the work. In the dwelling, however, where the parts are few, it stands but a single step in advance of uniformity, and is frequently displaced by symmetry. Downing defines this as that balance of opposite parts necessary to form an agreeable whole, but includes in it much we have assigned to regularity. A symmetrical building is balanced about a centre, or central plane, not by the exact correspondence of opposite members, but by a general equality of weight and power. With these definitions, the human form is regular; the well-formed tree is symmetrical. Regularity, in its somewhat sterner rule, may exist in the highest work, and does not altogether lose its power when it becomes the balancing of a few simple members. When regularity, either through the fewness or weakness of the parts, or through the want of any adequate reason for its somewhat mechanical arrangement, becomes barren, it may with advantage be displaced by symmetry. The purposes of domestic architecture require no exact balance of parts; indeed, more frequently they assign a new office, and hence a distinct form, to each distinct part.

As the edifice presents vertical and horizontal lines in constant contrast, and as the length of these in any given relation is not a matter of accident, but to be carefully determined by the purpose which unites them, there arises a demand for proportion. This we apprehend means no absolute relation of numbers to each other, implies no intrinsic agreement between dimensions, but rests solely on a right choice of length and breadth adapted to the particular end in view.

A dwelling will have beauty in proportion as it has character, and character is here an expression in all its forms, its adaptations of thought and feeling. The dwelling should not disguise itself under a false or a stereotyped form, but seek to be vocal, — to utter all its immediate purposes and relations. In obedience to this radical necessity of expression, —

(*a.*) The domestic edifice shows what it is, — a dwelling or a barn.

(*b.*) It shows what kind of a dwelling it is, — a farm-house, a cottage, a villa.

Country houses possess a great advantage over city houses. Their architecture is not reduced to a single surface: they have four instead of one or two sides. They are not compelled, through want of land, to spindle up into the air, but may occupy what space they choose. They have roofs, and not merely another floor. But country residences, as between themselves, have distinct objects. A farm-house has occasion to accommodate many and peculiar domestic operations. This fact it will take no pains to conceal, but will spread itself broadly on the ground, since the lower story is chiefly useful to it, and it possesses the land. The farmer's table is marked by its homely and abundant fare; his dwelling, by its many conveniences for various forms of domestic labor, and by its rural comforts.

The cottage — a term of vague application, but chiefly dependent on size, designating dwellings of moderate dimensions and vaguely involving some notion of taste — is in the country the house of men of limited means, whether of a mechanical or professional calling. It primarily provides for domestic wants, with a somewhat sparing recognition in the parlor of social enjoyments. It differs from the farm-house in making no provision for the production of any form of food, but only for its preparation for the table when furnished. These are the houses which belong to our villages, with a slim retinue of out-buildings, and an increasing height and value to the second story.

The villa designates a mansion, a larger form of

dwelling, and is usually in this country the home of the wealthy. Here the abuse of wealth commences, and yet there is a field which both taste and morals should be glad to recognize. The villa, so far as it is not the ostentatious effervescence of wealth, makes broader provision than the cottage for intellectual and social wants. The library, the drawing-room, and the tower become distinct features, and enjoyment gains ground upon simple living and labor. If this takes place to the exclusion of labor, a subordinate is reached in the destruction of a primary end. None can doubt that life may be rightly unfolded on its social and literary side, always providing that it falls not thereby into a vicious though fashionable indolence, into a useless though costly dilettanteism. These social forms of life, as shown in the dwelling, give it character, — enrich it by the manifold functions which it is seen to perform.

(*c.*) The dwelling should also receive character from its position, the objects in nature which surround it. In a warm climate and broad, sunny plains, it may be less compact, less sharp and angular, than in a rugged, mountainous region; may have more light, ample, and numerous verandas, and lie in the cool shade of deciduous trees. The home commanding valuable scenery will make provision, in tower, balcony, or veranda, for its enjoyment, and, occupying beautiful grounds, will have retired windows and sallying-points whence the inmates may go forth.

(*d.*) Another source of character in the dwelling is the transferred character of the inmate. Unfortunately the building more often suffers from this than is benefited by it, and in no way more frequently than by an ambitious attempt to secure architectural effect without adequate resources,—to transfer features that only appropriately belong to more costly work in a modified and flimsy form to cheaper material. The cottage thus loses the honest simplicity, the expression of homely comfort and self-respect, which belongs to it, and is made up of mean imitations, showing on the one side a foolish envy, on the other a foolish vanity.

If, however, honesty and simplicity characterize the builder, the building will often be favorably effected by the precise phase of his desires. Scarcely do any two families wish the same internal arrangement, the same variety and order of apartments, and with each new combination of wants there will appropriately and naturally be present a modified form. It is the province of every good artist, within the flexible arrangements of the given style of architecture, to express these individual types of social life. Nothing so intimately related to the family as the dwelling can rightly fail to receive form and character from it. All strong, rational life inevitably affects its instruments.

The true home, in the multiplicity of its offices, has a law for every part, an expression for every member, and if it falls short in the dignity of any one of these, it finds ample compensation in their variety and aggregate importance. Nor is the inside of the dwelling less fruitful in sources of character. Each room has a distinct object, and therein the basis of distinct treatment. No building, therefore, may be more individual, full, and human in its character than the dwelling,—the lodgement of thoughtful, emotional man.

Another most important and distinct class of buildings in protective architecture are those connected with religion. Many of the most costly and splendid edifices of all nations and countries have owed their origin to religion, and have been connected with worship. It is evident, that these edifices will receive character from the immediate purpose they are intended to subserve,—from the religion with which they stand connected and from national traits. A religion that receives its form from solemn ritual and costly ceremonial — which expresses its estimate of worship in visible gifts and manual work — will put forth its strength, ingenuity, and feeling to rear a temple, or temples, adorned with all that the most expensive architecture can confer. In such a faith, the temple is the emblem, the embodiment of worship, and as such must not lack anything which an aroused heart and free hand can give. So stood the Jewish temple, in its rich magnificence a religious work, reverence and faith transmuted into stone and the precious metals. On the other hand, as a religion forsakes the visible for the invisible, the formal for the spiritual, its edifices sink from the necessities of worship to the conveniences of worship, from direct religious gifts to God, carrying the heart over in actual recognition and adoration, to an antecedent preparation, having its end, not in worship, but in the wants of worshippers. Such are Christian churches. They do not embody the worship of those who worship in them, nor express their sense of what man should render to God: they are a social and religious instrument for a social and religious end, and are to be judged as means in fulfilling this end.

Aside from the direct object of a religious edifice, it is evident that the general spirit of the religion, as developed in the faith and lives of those who rear the church, will impart to it certain corresponding qualities.

Reverence and fear, slightly tinctured with love and hope, will heap up solemn, grand, and gloomy piles, where the heart worships, yet a great way off from its God; where the feelings can only rise and fall with the slow, measured surge of the organ. A faith which puts slight restraint on its votaries, whose new birth is under the lead of old notions, will in its religious edifices develop the same pride, exclusion, love of cost and display which may chance to characterize its wealthy adherents in their personal expenditures. Or, perchance, a cultivated taste and intense love of art will baptize itself into a religious name, and strictly under its old impulses, become at its new altar the devotee of architecture. On the other hand, a faith which is born into the kingdom of Christ will in every act remember that his kingdom is not of this world, — will in all that it does show a superior and controlling sense of spiritual relations and religious duties. The costly cathedrals of the old world, and their imitations with us, admirable as may be their workmanship, we apprehend, have sprung out of an impure Christian faith, and cannot purely, rightly, beautifully embody a faith which rests on Christ of Calvary.

These works, so grand in themselves and oftentimes so truly related to the untrue, or rather partial, faith which gave rise to them, have necessarily drawn forth much devotion from students of art, — have inclined them to overlook the fact that they find no place in the simplicity of the Christian ritual, and to treat but scornfully any criticism which rejects these edifices as untrue to Christian character. We shall sternly insist on the principle of subordination, that pre-eminently in the field of her own architecture is the law of religion superior to the law of beauty, or rather, that beauty only exists in the perfect fulfilment of the law and spirit of religion. Before, therefore, we can pronounce the cathedral an appropriate or inappropriate form of church edifice, we must know the purpose of the Protestant Church, the religious spirit which expresses itself in it. That church is the most beautiful which most truly contains and utters that spirit. The edifice cannot be separated from its purpose and the true character of its worshippers, but must, as by induction, receive this purpose and share this character.

(*a.*) A church is strictly an assembly-room for a social end, — worship. In many climates, the stately dimensions and the high, vaulted roofs of Gothic churches are not fitted for comfort, and do not meet the very end of protection which instituted them. They are not auditories, having feeble adaptations either for speaker or hearer. They do not inspire that cheerful and sympathetic feeling which should belong to an audience of Christian neighbors, and involve an expense altogether beyond that requisite to meet the real ends of the edifice. In thus overlooking the highest comfort of the audience, and the very fact that it is an audience, inspiring feelings more or less alien to cheerful faith, they override the religious end which calls them forth with an æsthetical end of their own, and thus, in their unfitness, are no more beautiful churches than they would be beautiful dwellings.

(*b.*) Regarded as the exhibition of private generosity, they are as often the medium of pride as of genuine benevolence.

(*c.*) The very proprieties and associations of these costly edifices invite to lavish expenditure in dress, and are thus increasingly liable to become the exclusive possession of those who can afford an expensive Gospel. The crowning proof of Christianity is thus lost, — the poor have the Gospel preached unto them. The atmosphere of the place becomes one of ease, affluence, self-indulgence, wholly alien to the humility, self-denial, and love which are the peculiar, the working forces of the new and spiritual kingdom of Christ. The difficulty lies in the spirit of the place and of the audience, — a spirit which manifests itself in the ostentatious architecture, the rich, gloomy grandeur of the edifice, in the costly garments, in the cold propriety and courtly dignity of the audience. There is no self-denial, no condescension, no humility anywhere manifest: the people are in no sense a "peculiar people," unless it be for their universal display of wealth.

Such a temper, so far as it prevails, first enervates, then destroys Christianity. The catholic breadth, humility, and thus grandeur, of its work should be written in most legible characters on the lintels and doorposts of all its structures. The manger and the cathedral are a long way apart, not less in spirit than in form. The one speaks of a kingdom and glory laid aside, the other of it resumed; the one, of the invisible overruling the visible and banishing it, the other of the visible once more striving to draw back and imprison in its pomp and majesty the invisible; the one walks by faith, the other by sight. The cathedral is neither inference, application, nor improvement of the text, "My kingdom is not of this world." The massive cathedral, with its echoing arches and unfathomed recesses, makes fitting response to the mystic rites of Popery, but the quick, sympathetic love of the Christian heart is congealed in its cold shadow.

(*d.*) The expense of these edifices precludes their use as Christian churches. In a world for the most part destitute of churches, the Christian and missionary spirit must be identical. Every effort must have reference to conquest, and that which shows indolence, weakness of desire, a willingness to tarry amid private enjoyments, a partial and hesitating surrender of resources to the only effort known to Christianity, denies the cross and the gospel of self-sacrifice. We first suffer with Christ, and afterward reign with him. Costly architecture reigns by anticipation, reigns without Christ, and, by its premature prodigality, loses its right to reign with him. It is yet the hour of labor in which indulgence is treachery, and labor and love, not repose, must be written on the church, as on every other tablet of our faith. Christianity — a spiritual democracy — must have faith in its own broad principles, in its own humility, and feel that all which limits it, concentrates it, gathers it up into classes, establishments, institutions, edifices, by making it partial, makes it poor and weak for its world-wide work.

That church architecture is best which has most of inspiration in it, of Christian, Christ-like character, of cheerful, inclusive love, of self-denial, of the invisible reigning over and reigning in the visible under the type of Calvary. It should be a true, pure representation of the Christian spirit, not towering in the midst of poverty with ostentatious luxury, not vaunting its costly decorations while men perish of spiritual destitution, but cheerful, free, serviceable, and under these conditions tasteful, inviting and entertaining all with

Christian accord. An expensive church, in the light of the demand which the world is everywhere making for money, cannot stand as a fitting expression of the Christian spirit; it is at best but the utterance of Christian pride or Christian forgetfulness.

A third form of protective architecture, giving full play to the artist's power, calling for noble and stable forms, and justifying large expenditure, are public buildings. These express the strength, stability, and wealth of a nation; and a nation does well to lend itself liberally to the public service. Colleges, all institutions of learning, in their intrinsic value and durability, in the claim which may be made upon them for good taste, and as representing our devotion to knowledge, furnish appropriate fields for the most various architecture. The noblest styles of the past, Grecian and Gothic, may reappear in the service of knowledge and of government.

Architecture of support is so restricted and so thoroughly utilitarian in its office as rarely to appear in the field of fine arts. The bridge and aqueduct are its best structures.

Commemorative architecture, on the other hand, is slightly ruled by utility. Permanence is the leading law of form, and within this limit all appropriate and beautiful expression may be sought. This very freedom renders fine monuments difficult of attainment, and they need as far as possible to be individualized by the character of the particular event intrusted to them.

Having reviewed some of the resources and aims of architecture, we need to speak of a distinct, subordinate element it frequently employs,—ornament. Ornamentation may vary form within the limits of use, or it may occupy with work of its own void spaces, thus imparting additional fulness and interest to the edifice. This ornament will always be subsidiary in its relations and in the impression it makes upon the mind. The general outline, character, and office of the edifice will first occupy attention, and only later, when partially satisfied, will the mind turn to the details of treatment, and glean the pleasure of ornament, — the completion of what is in itself noble.

(*a.*) The carving of ornament will rarely be complete, but rather be suggestive and symbolical, drawn from those forms of life which most readily admit this treatment. This results from the rough character of the material which receives its work, being the surfaces which the building itself may afford; from the permanent and often exposed position of the product; from the rude chiselling of ordinary workmen who are to be employed; and from the facts, that the building as a whole, and not its parts, is the object of the artist, that careful imitation in unpliant and coarse material is less pleasing than bold strokes, and that the cost of the edifice will not suffer that each member should be made a separate subject of fine art.

Architecture does not, even in its ornament, infringe the domain of sculpture. The one is rapid and representative, the other accurate and presentative. The architect, while not content to leave his stone entirely blank, does not wish to cut any member into so high an effect as to destroy its character as a subordinate feature, while the sculptor expends his whole power on a single thing, and makes it the great and costly product of his art. The architect works through many agents, and leaves a product great in mass, though weak in separate members; the sculptor works alone, and leaves a product small in mass, but condensed and potent in expression.

(*b.*) The ornament of the architect will grow elaborate and careful in proportion as the position assigned it is sheltered and near at hand. Wise art shows economy by giving its rough chiselling to exposed parts, and by treating its work in size and finish according to the height of the position from which it is to present itself. This is to adapt the object to the end to be reached.

(*c.*) According as the architect has given fulness, variety, and force to the outline of his building without and within, will the work of ornamentation be obvious and easy. In a form already fruitful, it becomes wholly secondary, and readily occupies the limited spaces left it. On the other hand, if the building is barren in design, the most judicious ornament will still leave it feeble in expression, and the difficulty of reaching this ornament will be found proportionately great.

This is well illustrated in the ceiling of a large hall. If the architecture has made nothing of it, but left it one blank surface, the utmost skill of decoration will but partially repair the defect. In architecture, as elsewhere, the less the reliance placed on ornament, the more strictly it remains secondary, the greater will be the vigor and power of the work. Amid the earnest workings of thought, adapting limited resources to unyielding ends, ornament comes in as the transient play of passing feelings, — the affection with which the mind executes its conceptions.

Architecture and gardening of all the fine arts are of the most broad and practical interest. Here especially is the popular taste awakened and cultivated. A painting or statuette poorly atones for a desolate dwelling and dreary yards. The beauty of a country, as well as the taste of its inhabitants, will depend chiefly on these two arts, and these alone render appropriate the presence of the higher and more condensed products of beauty. Beauty intertwines itself by root and stem with these utilities of our common life, and later bears as blossoms the choice labors of high art.

A class of structures that have received the earliest and most continuous attention are those connected with religion. The progress and forms of architecture can be more easily and exactly traced in connection with these than with any other edifices. The chief architectural feature of the Egyptian temple was the colonnade. This surrounded one or more courts, and formed the front of the temple proper. The interior rooms of the temple, the cell and its ante-chambers, were inconsiderable and inconspicuous parts of the architecture. In general outline, the temple of Solomon was not unlike those of Egypt. The Egyptian column was massive, not fitted in form with precision to its office, and placed at short intervals. The general impression was, therefore, heavy and gloomy. One wandered between huge pillars, rather than entered into open, cheerful spaces. The support was excessive and somewhat clumsy.

In the Grecian and Roman temple, the colonnade still remained the chief feature, though its arrangement was different. Instead of enclosing a court, it ran across the front of the edifice, or, as in the Parthenon, entirely surrounded it. The Grecian temple was built for the outside rather than the inside. Its chief impression was the exterior one, produced by its series of columns. These now received the most elegant and precise forms, and, with wider spaces, yielded adequate but not superabundant support. The impression of a Greek temple was chiefly due to its horizontal lines. From these the vertical lines started, and in them they terminated. The spaces to be spanned were broad: the frieze, therefore, having to sustain a corresponding pressure, became proportionately broad. A plain surface, just beneath the projection of the cornice, it became a favorite and sheltered position for carved ornament, encircling the entire building. In this respect it had no rival except the pediments at each end. The column, with its base and capital, became in Grecian art so symmetrical, so exactly fitted in form to its office, so proportionate, and so beautifully united to the grand ornate masses that rested upon it, that skill could go no farther in this direction. This order of architecture was complete, perfect; and progress must come with a change of idea.

The Roman furnished the conception that was to give this new direction. The arch was not unknown to previous, to Egyptian art; but it had not subserved any conspicuous or important purpose. The false arch, chiefly employed in India, has not the essential characteristic of the arch. The pressure in it is wholly vertical, the stones sustaining each other by their breadth: the upper ones overlap the lower ones, and at length, from each side, meet at the summit. The arch was first used, and chiefly used, by the Romans in connection with Greek features of architecture, and thus gave a mingled style known as Romanesque. We shall understand this best in connection with Christian churches. These churches grew in form out of the Roman basilica, — a court of justice and a place for popular assemblies. The basilica, in the Greek form, was a quadrangle enclosed by a colonnade; was faced without at one end by a colonnade, while the opposite interior end was occupied by the tribune. A ground-plan of such a structure is easily given by a quadrangle whose length is double its breadth, whose interior is surrounded by a series of dots indicating the columns that divide the side-aisles from the centre, and whose front is faced by another series of dots indicative of the porch. The centre of this structure was either left open; or upon the entablature that crowned the columns of the two side-aisles was erected a wall extending up a second story, pierced in the upper portion for light, and giving support to a flat, panelled ceiling. The basilica in this form was easily made to fulfil the purposes of a church. It soon, however, under Christian sentiment, underwent these changes. That the ground-plan might present the figure of a cross, the transept was introduced. The intersection of this with the main part of the building — the nave — became the centre of the structure. Just beyond this, the head of the cross was occupied by the great altar and the choir. The nave and the transepts had each their side-aisles, and each furnished entrance to the building. The altar and choir were flanked on either side by aisles in continuation of those of the nave, and which united in a polygonal apse in the rear. The high altar, thus occupying one end of the church, impressed such a character on it as to lead at length to placing it toward the east, thus leaving the grand entrance toward the west. Such was the form the church slowly assumed under the influence of a growing Catholicism.

If we enter a Greek basilica church, as that of Marie

Maggiore, or that of St. Paul, at Rome, we are impressed by the horizontal character of the structure. As we stand in the nave, a broad, horizontal ceiling lies far above us; and on either hand stretch away the heavy entablatures that crown the rows of receding Grecian pillars. We also observe that the interior of the building has become very impressive, — more so than the exterior; and that, in this respect, it differs decidedly from Pagan religious art. The arch may be introduced into such a structure in various ways. It may be placed between the columns under the entablatures, which it thus aids in supporting. In that case, the simple column does not afford sufficient attachment and support to the foot of the arch, and is therefore replaced by a mass of masonry faced beneath each arch by a pilaster reaching up to and sustaining it, and in front by a pilaster extending up to the entablature. If this feature is carried through the structure, the ceiling is vaulted throughout, and the windows and doors are round-headed. Thus from a Grecian cornice there rises a semicircular ceiling, lifted high enough to command independent light above the vaulted aisles.

The impression of such a church, of which St. Peter's is an example, is quite different from that of a Greek basilica. In St. Peter's, the massive masonry, which, taking the place of columns, divides the aisles from the nave, serves to detach them very much from the body of the church, and would do so still more, were it not for the great height and breadth of the included arches. A Romanesque church has less unity and less singleness of impression than either a Greek or Gothic one. The aisles are more detached; the horizontal line is broken, yet not abolished. A most striking advantage of this style is the ease and grace with which it receives a dome at the intersection of the nave and transept. The semi-circular arches readily support a circular entablature; and above this rises the hemispherical dome. When the Latin cross is changed into the Greek cross, and the central dome is surrounded by minor domes covering the sections of the transept and nave, as in St. Mark's at Venice, the Romanesque passes into the Byzantine style.

The plain vaulting of the ceiling and of the dome also furnishes favorite surfaces for decoration, for fresco. These paintings are often very elaborate, — more so, it seems to us, than their position justifies. A simple and bold effect, placed at so dizzy a height, is the easiest, to say the least, of apprehension by the observer.

We are now close to Gothic architecture in the progress of thought, though still far from it in the general impression and character of the work under consideration. Having spanned the windows with a round arch, it was easy to substitute for it, in the solid wall, a pointed arch. The suggestion might then arise of carrying this form of the arch into all parts of the building. This idea completed gives us Gothic architecture. The pointed arch could not easily, fittingly, be crowded down under the Greek entablature. Its sharp apex afforded no appropriate support to it; came up as if to pierce it rather than to sustain it, and was out of harmony with it. Moreover, this arch itself, as much higher than the circular arch, could not find room beneath the architrave, and must be left at liberty to expand itself above it. Farther: this arch, as higher, required a corresponding height in the column on which it rested, and for this reason the more must break through the superincumbent mass above. On these grounds, the chief Grecian feature of the building disappeared entirely. Nor could the Grecian column advantageously remain with the new arch. This sloped so gently, as the foot was approached, that it readily united itself directly to the pillar beneath, without the distinct support that had been demanded by the round-headed arch. Moreover, as each column was the central support of many arches, the groins of these passed freely into the column, and lay upon its surface, giving it the appearance of a cluster of smaller columns compactly wrought into a larger one. This pillar thus ceased to be Grecian in form, and had no occasion for the Grecian capital. It either had no capital, or one peculiar to it.

The whole expression of the building is now changed. All its lines are vertical, and terminate with a slight curve upward. The unity of the structure is much greater than before. The clustered column takes the place of a mass of masonry, and gives the minimum support possible. The height of the church is relatively greater than it could be under the former style. Not only is the sharp arch higher in itself, and in its column, than the round arch, but its lateral thrust is much less; and there is, therefore, no mechanical difficulty in giving these upward tendencies full development. In a structure stone throughout, the lateral pressure is, in connection with the arch, the most serious difficulty to be met. The Romans, indeed, used such excellent cement, and loaded their walls and arches so heavily, as seen in the Baths of Caracalla, as almost to destroy the character of the arch as a mechanical device. Many of these arches were as independent and self-supporting as if they had been cut out of solid rock. When large spaces were to be spanned in a lighter way, and at great height, the thrust of the arch was a most formidable obstacle, as shown by the many cracked and seamed walls visible in less fortunate structures. The Gothic arch was peculiarly adapted to meet this difficulty, and that, too, in connection, as we have seen, with great height. Suppose that a wall a hundred feet high is to be made the foot of an arch, reaching, with a span of sixty feet, a corresponding wall. If we were striving simply to answer the inquiry, How shall this wall be so strengthened as to resist the lateral pressure put upon it? this method would be easily hit upon: Build a second wall thirty-five feet in the rear, parallel with the first, and half its height. Unite these, at intervals of thirty feet, with cross-walls, passing through the outer and lower wall, and appearing externally as buttresses, and rising on the inner and higher wall as supports to the distance of seventy-five feet. Let the buttresses of the lower wall be crowned with pinnacles, and, from a point near the base of these, let flying supports or buttresses, in the form of a slight arch, whose ends rest at unequal heights, pass up to the inner wall, reaching it somewhat above the middle of that portion, twenty-five feet in breadth, which remains unsupported. Is it not evident that our inner wall can now receive with ease and safety a severe lateral pressure? And this is the construction of a Gothic church, with the unimportant difference, that the higher wall and connecting walls are pierced within and beneath by arches, and supported by columns, thus making way for the passage of the aisle, and putting it in connection with the nave. If we have, as in the Milan Cathedral, two aisles on either side, instead of one, then we have three supporting walls, instead of two.

The Gothic cathedral thus shows a perfect adaptation of all its external members and ornaments to architectural purposes: they all perform some service, and spring from some mechanical ground or occasion. Such a building is as striking without as within: the exterior and interior vie with each other in power and beauty. The variety of parts and relations is very great in both. Were it not for the perfect unity of the structure, the eye would be lost and bewildered in the multiplicity of members. Yet the ninety-eight pinnacles of the Milan Cathedral, by the uniformity and simplicity of their mechanical arrangement and functions, escape all confusion, and add, in a simple way, their wonderful variety to the single and grand structure.

The Greek temple, as the Parthenon, and the Gothic cathedral, as that of Cologne, stand at the two extremes of the art: the one has the simplicity and repose of strength; the other the variety, manifold resources, and startling execution of the most intense aspiration. The mind is borne upward till lost in the marvellous skill of the work and the dizziness of the heights attained. At each retreat, the buttress still stretches up; once at its summit, the taper pinnacle crowns it, and this stands out against the background of the still climbing roof studded with higher pinnacles; while above all, towers one or more spires, holding to the eye a swimming, uncertain height against the floating clouds beyond. Aspiration, splendid achievement, are stamped on every feature of such an edifice, and can scarcely go farther. Cologne Cathedral, if once finished, would be a marvel of another kind, nowise second to the Parthenon.

The power of Gothic architecture is also shown in the manner in which it rejects ornament beyond its own structural features. Within, the vaulted and groined ceiling is sufficient unto itself, and offers no spaces for painting. The decorations of color find their seat in the stained glass of the windows; and the gorgeous effect which these produce leaves the architecture intact. In some cases, the exterior has been prodigally adorned with sculpture. Of this the Cathedral of Milan is the most marked illustration. Its statues are numbered by thousands. In their prodigality and inaccessibility, they show a false subordination of a higher to a lower art, and a vulgar effort to impress by quantity. Moreover, the building owes very little to them. Robbed of them all, it would still retain its chief power.

One feature of the Romanesque style, and that, too, the finest, — the dome, — finds no place in the Gothic church. A vaulted chamber or lantern sometimes takes its position; with no considerable effect, however. As the intersection of the transept and nave is not the fitting position for the leading spire, even this feeble substitute cannot often be introduced. A heavy tower at this point unduly burdens, rides, the building, is unserviceable as a bell-tower, and adorns a portion of the edifice already sufficiently interesting. The tower or towers at the west end, on the other hand, subserve a mechanical purpose in closing and firmly uniting the walls, readily hold the bells, give balance to the structure by adding interest to an otherwise remote and unsustained portion, and furnish that beautiful outline which belongs to a spire starting independently from the very ground. The Gothic church excludes the dome, or should do so, by virtue of the incongruity of the pointed arch with its circular outlines. The Romanesque style belongs more especially to Italy; the Gothic to Northern Italy, to France and the Rhine, and to England.

Styles of architecture may be said to differ in the manner in which they bridge or cover their open spaces, — that from side-wall to side-wall, that from column to column, those of the door and the window. The Grecian style does this by a horizontal line or surface; the Gothic by a pointed curve; other styles do it by intermediate and mingled forms. In some more modern structures, one form, the semicircular arch, has been singled out, divested of all other features of style, and made the initial idea of the entire building. The result is more peculiar and interesting than that reached by any of the mixed methods. This style may be called round-headed Gothic, and as a pure, complete style is modern.

In domestic architecture, the Swiss seem to have achieved as distinct a style as any European nation. The Swiss châlet, in its artistic forms, is a cosey, modest, attractive house, and bespeaks cheerful snugness and domestic comfort. It is, doubtless, connected in expression with the moderate circumstances and generally-developed character of the inhabitants of most of the cantons. The Norman villa is also an edifice of a decided, though a much more aristocratic character. Its high step-gables, round tower, and angles fortified with circular pinnacles, present a bold and varied outline, and unite themselves to large dimensions. The French or Mansard roof is another national feature of architecture. Aside from these forms, there is little interesting or peculiar in the domestic architecture of Europe. Brick, with varying forms and color, appears in some fine buildings; for instance, the City Hall at Berlin.

LECTURE XIV.

SCULPTURE.—VALUE OF THE TRUTH PRESENTED.—CHOICE OF SUBJECTS.—HISTORIC ART.—RANGE OF SCULPTURE.—REPOSE MATERIAL.—FORM.—PURE FORM.

In sculpture we reach the representative arts. These do not subserve a physical, but a spiritual end. No demand of mere utility is met by the reproduction of natural objects,—by the statue or the painting. All the physical exigencies of life have reference to facts, and not to their reflections, however beautiful. These arts address themselves to the mind, and their value lies in the sentiments which they communicate. Great truths cannot be too laboriously or assiduously uttered. The more lasting, impressive, and perfect the form which they assume, the better; for they are the landmarks of all generations, the beacons which make the pathless sea,—whereon all crafts freighted with nations, the rich argosy, the warlike trireme, the steamship and the bark canoe, sailing up from the mysterious horizon of the past, press onward,—as safe as the rutted road.

As beauty lies in the manner an independent end is reached, the truth which representative art brings forward must itself be both obvious and important. If obscurely presented, it has but little hold on the intellect, and less upon the heart. If unimportant, it cannot justify the labor expended or the attention invited. This is true of painting, and, in a yet higher degree, of sculpture. A good painting involves great labor, and can present but one scene. A poem with relative ease presents many scenes. The first, therefore, as more laborious in its methods and limited in the range of its results, can only appropriately employ itself on the more potent and pregnant passages of life. Thus, though uttering one thing and delivering one message, the good painting never falls back among unfortunate and pretentious, or suffers itself to be overlooked among neglected, commonplaces. This fate it can only escape by working up powerfully important sentiment. The more laboriously a trite truth is presented the more intolerable is it. The familiar seeks a familiar, rapid, and transient utterance; the weighty alone can come forward to occupy grave moments, to invite our deliberate and repeated contemplation. The painting is not wiped out, is not modified, but, year by year, must rest its claim to attention, to existence, on its first, its only, its intrinsic truth. This is a severe test, excluding the trivial not less than the false. What art strives to make permanent she must first be sure is valuable. If our taste is so blind and unfortunate as to attach value to anything in which the mind and heart have no portion, it robs us of our only relief, destruction, and surrounds us forever with weak and worn-out products, the fatal fecundity of an unripe fancy; this, too, in the very teeth of Nature, who is ever changing her products, who paints only to destroy and repaint, who suffers the most brilliant sunset to fade into darkness, and is ever returning to an azure sky, that she may begin again her cloud-work, who sends the besom of winter to brush clean her canvas, and who each day retouches her previous labors. Even the most powerful utterances of truth in men and actions are not long continued, but are ever arising under some new form with a new shading of circumstances and new conditions of character. Great men and great events are not repeated, are not prints struck from the same plate, and little events in their constant flux make up the shifting stream of time.

In a yet higher degree is this strict limitation to emphatic truths suitable to sculpture. Demanding even more time than painting to realize its products, having much less variety of truth intrusted to it, a most costly and chaste art, it can only do a valuable work when animated with a high sense of the office to which it is called, of the nature of the work which is worthy of it. We can do without statues, but what shall we do with feeble and indecent ones? This is a dilemma from which there is no relief without either a cruel waste of labor or of taste or of morals. Garments, furniture, houses, wear out, and the mistakes of fancy cease to torture us and give place to others; but an unfortunate statue, alas! can stand in its speechless nothingness, a pitiable mute forever, too much of man in it to be broken, too little of man in it to be enthroned as a power in any human heart. It can only linger on in dingy, dusty existence, waiting the charity of accident, durability being, in the sad catalogue of its qualities, the most sad.

The time which the execution of a statue requires, the attention which it claims, the limited scope of the truth which it presents, and its durability, all demand that it should perpetuate only the higher, nobler, and more profound sentiments of our nature, that it should be well aware that truth, great truth, and only truth, is committed to it, that it is the vault of our treasures, the casket of our jewels. What we are not willing to let die, we seal within stone lips, too full of their message not to utter it, too full of their message to utter it all, — sphinx-lips that speak to the light.

The principle which has been termed the dignity of beauty here exerts a most important influence.

(*a.*) Between physical and spiritual qualities, the ripeness of organic structure and character, the latter only is worthy of the chisel. The embalmed body, in spite of Egyptian myrrhs, becomes a mummy. As, however, the soul finds most perfect expression in a perfect body, it is the physical as transfigured by the spiritual which is the true theme of sculpture. Nude statuary throws the whole weight of its peculiar effect into the balance of our baser nature, and thus wars with the true end of high art.

(*b.*) Facts, as contrasted with ideas, have a peculiar claim on the sculptor. History, as compared with myths and vagaries of a credulous or a classical fancy, has a superior hold upon truth, and thus upon art.

(1.) Such work at once renders an adequate reason why it is, by defining its utility and the office which it subserves. Virtue is honored, the memory and power of great deeds kept alive, and the echo of past achievement made clear and ringing in the present. This is for the world to show itself grateful, and still more wise, treasuring up the moral power of the past as the working force of the present. Commemorative statues have a most obvious and just end wholly aside from beauty, and thus that basis in which true beauty can inhere.

(2.) These products of art have also correspondingly more of expression. There is a history known to all back of them, and this history consolidated in character comes forth in them. Here is common ground for the artist and for the critic or recipient of art. The one must know the time and the man, and rightly embody these, while the other may also have the interpreting knowledge with which to reach all that the artist thought and felt. Every face gathers meaning and expression by our knowledge of the man, and the true key of the statue are the historic events which gave rise to it and which it utters. In proportion as these are not merely the private experience of an individual, but great facts for the world, will the resulting work have interest and power. It thus stands as on a triumphal column, marking epochs in the march of man. So, too, the gratitude and loyalty to virtue, which these most apt and faithful remembrancers indicate, will heighten their expression.

(3.) The very limitation under which such art must work out its conception should rather be regarded as an advantage than a disadvantage. History, in preserving the general cast of features which belonged to her favored actors, gives a valuable law and restraint to the work of reproduction. To infuse the true, the requisite character into these, then, becomes the problem, and strong art will rejoice in it. This is an incarnation, the enshrining of a divine spirit in veritable flesh. Good historic work stands rooted in facts, and will be kept fresh and forceful as long as the memory of man loves to linger on the records of the race.

(*c.*) In imaginative work, single virtues have an advantage over more general and inclusive conceptions. A single virtue gives more distinctness and point to character, secures a more free and independent variety, and saves the product from vague generalization. There is here, also, a key to the work,— that by which the artist may be understood, that by which he may be judged: we seek for a powerful grouping of the visible symbols of a single predominant emotion. Beauty here becomes a tribute to virtue. Virtue is seen working itself out in beauty.

Of the same nature are the personifications of distinct and characteristic portions of time, of the morning or evening, of summer or spring, of youth or age. These phases of existence may be made personal in their striking features, and be gathered up in a beautiful symbol. Here are found some of the most signal achievements of sculpture.

It may be said that a good statue is its own chart, and that it is a sad caricature which needs the interpretation of a label. While this is in part true, we can, nevertheless, understand and enjoy the artist only as he travels in a distinct and decided way toward a definite object, through ground the habitat of human feeling. The quicker and more thoroughly we find out what he is at, the better; the more distinct, positive, and apprehensible the end to be realized, the better. The mind of the artist is strung to an effort, and we know nothing till we know the object of that effort. Its aim cannot be some great and beautiful effect, but must be a particular expression, a definite beauty. However we, as spectators, arrive at the end, it must first be reached before the work is understood or wisely enjoyed.

Sculpture, from the costliness of the art, is bound to choose the nobler themes. It will find these in man. Man is its chief, well-nigh its exclusive subject. This also arises from the only symbol at its disposal,— form. The vegetable form cannot meet the mechanical conditions of sculpture, cannot sustain itself in stone, and is too little expressive to become an object of this art. Animal life is of so feeble a character, is so little on the surface, is so overlaid with shell and hair and hide, as to make no considerable figure in sculpture, aside from immediate connection with man.

On the other hand, the smooth uncovered skin of man, undulatory and minutely expressive, with the soul on the surface, makes him a fit subject for an art dealing only with the single symbol, form. Even man, however, must be dealt with singly or in simple limited relations, as in the equestrian statue. From this restricted range of the art there are several results.

(*a.*) Vice, though under the form of retribution, cannot well become a subject for the chisel. Such figures need to be explained and overborne in their effect by the presence and triumph of virtue. They are only acceptable as features in a somewhat complex whole, and such a group sculpture cannot render. I know not how a Laocoön writhing in the toils of a serpent is to be called beautiful. Such a use of words must at least demand a transfer of sympathy from the man to the snake. Human agony is in itself considered terrible, not beautiful. The mind cannot rest with pleasure on a scene of agony, however powerfully rendered. We will not say that the only thing to be rendered is beauty, — but that this torture of the heart is not beauty.

(*b.*) Virtue must present itself in the form of repose, trenched in native strength rather than in violent action. Such action requires again explanation. A solid stone statue frowning on an imaginary enemy seems haunted with some ghost of guilt and danger which will not down. That which is to be perpetual and alone should be peaceful. The imagination will hardly make the figures to which the passion of a statue responds so stand out in real existence as to render pleasing the effect. If an angry general, rebuking his retreating soldiers, were left as the only figure in a painting, we should hardly retain it long scowling into vacancy, but put even second rate art to service to reclaim for it a few runaways. The human face, in the armed or trustful repose of virtuous strength, is the citadel of sculpture.

(*c.*) Here also we mark a further distinction between the carving of the architect and the cutting of the sculptor. Every form of life sustained by the solid stone beneath is open to the one, while man is the leading, if not the only theme of the other. Even in bas-relief, sculpture still shows its adhesion to high truth, to man. Architecture also often symbolizes and distorts its work. It is not content with, nor does it aim at, the truthful, but intensifies and makes glaring the prominent expression, striving to throw into the deadness of the brute something of the passion of the man. Sculpture, on the other hand, is satisfied with the fulness of the truth committed to it, and aims at that alone.

There is a spirit in man, and the inspiration of the Almighty giveth them understanding. This is the starting and returning point of sculpture, the basis and substance of all it has to say. Within this circle of human powers it works, nor finds itself straitened. Its material and means are as simple and restricted as its end. Pure, spotless marble is its chosen, its almost exclusive material. Bronze in rougher and more exposed work is the only important exception, and here the perfection of the art proportionately suffers. Bold and striking, rather than exquisite and finished, the bronze statue looks down upon you from a height, and stands in the cold sleet without moving sympathy.

The single symbol of expression in sculpture is form, and this fact shows how thoroughly this is the basis of every other symbol. Color, shade, and motion are all dependent upon it, while it is independent of each. Form puts us in direct connection with thought, is the explicit and immediate utterance of thought. Where, and in what language can so full a chapter be written, so deep a discovery of emotion be made, as in the features of a statue which your hand might hide? The spring of life from which the poet is always drawing here comes welling up to the surface. The passions, desires, hopes, with which the tongue is ever employed here lie in silent, constant, condensed utterance, the impress of mind on matter, the great marvel of the invisible wrought into the visible, working out its every power in appreciable form.

Motion, through the suggestion of attitude, may be thought to be a subsidiary symbol of sculpture. This in a slight degree it is. But the statue usually existing alone, and therefore relatively in repose, motion becomes a less significant adjunct than in painting, and can hardly be regarded as a distinct symbol.

Nothing in art equals the purity, the singleness, the chastity of sculpture, — human emotion in colorless marble. The statue may at first seem cold and cheerless in its tranquil pallor, and yet it cannot depart from this, its high throne of pure form, without loss. The tinged marble may look more like flesh, may, like waxwork, have more of resemblance, but, in stooping to secure this, it has lost the simple dignity of its first message.

I know few more significant facts in art than the growth upon the heart of the colorless statue, and the feeling akin to sacrilege which is occasioned by any, even the most perfect tincture. Art has by instinct almost uniformly rejected any such effort, and, though not always knowing why, has felt the ground already possessed to be higher.

(*a.*) It illustrates what has been said of resemblance as not constituting the aim of art. It is here not even concurrent with art, and we gain it with a decided loss of power. With each stroke of color we seem to descend from pure and transcendental truth toward commonplace fact.

(*b.*) It is also an instance of governed and restrained emotion. We like to see the sculptor accept and cling to the stern but natural law of his art, to reject that which is extrinsic, which is of the nature of ornament, and to be content with the noble simplicity of truth. We are reluctant to see a purity so marked mingle with the common crowd of colored things, overlook its own distinct and individual nature, and strive to lose itself in the generic type. As the mind gains in culture, it eagerly accepts this new restraint, and loves the statue all the more because it is by so much less than the painting. It wishes to see it so great in its own most grand prerogative as not to covet color.

(*c.*) There is here an illustration of the desire that every material should adhere to its own nature. Marble is not a good canvas, and in so using it we hide a most adequate, beautiful, and native surface with one wholly alien.

(*d.*) The mind's delight in distinction and analysis is shown in the statue. We like to see what is due to form anatomized out from every other symbol of expression, — to have the power of this single symbol revealed. All that compounds the impression and returns it to the common channel takes from it the keen relish of an analytic and intelligent pleasure.

(*e*.) Undoubtedly the power of association is here also shown. The purity of white lends a certain chastity and vigor to the emotions which widely sunder them from those of amorous flesh. A sacred innocence veils the work, making it to the heart more holy.

These considerations together give to sculpture a more delicate, refined, and subtile character than belongs to any other art, and make the statue the chaste repose of virtue, — the calm strength of a pure spirit. From this its high character statuary should all the more be subject to the law of utility, and not degenerate into simple and idle ornament. Let the end of influence, something to be uttered, something to be honored, some truth again to be restored to the light, show how and why and where it shall be present. This neglected, and the most pertinent and immediate of all inquiries is overlooked, and statues are more aimless than the flocking clouds speeding each to its ministration.

How immortal is that which is most precious in man! The earnest thought brooding into symmetrical, ideal loveliness the forces of the human soul, the cunning hand waking from its repose in the virgin marble a pure, permanent semblance, together enthrone this solemn, silent life on its stone pedestal, — an angelic voice, audible in all time to all hearts.

LECTURE XV.

PAINTING. — TRUTH. — VIRTUE. — DIGNITY. — MANNER OF TREAT MENT. — THEMES. — MAN. — NATURE. — SYMBOLS. — COLOR LIGHT, MOTION. — POWERS REQUISITE IN PAINTERS.

PAINTING has always been one of the most widely cultivated and generally influential of the fine arts. It includes a greater variety of subjects than any art save poetry, and is more precise and full in its presentations than even poetry. The visible is the great field of beauty. It is thought realized, and not abstract relations, that gives rise to this sentiment. But the visible world is throughout open to painting. All that the eye sees and the imagination constructs the painter may present. The whole sweep of facts and of ideals — the growth of facts — lies before him. The accurate, literal, and fixed rendering to which the painting is bound may sometimes limit it, but is also its power. Though the angelic and supernatural enter with more reluctance and danger the sphere of visible art than the field of the poetic imagination, less distinct and definite in its suggestion, the real and the ideal, its fulfilment, rejoice in this perfect presentation which makes of them a full and visible fact. The power of painting is due not less to the precision than to the variety of its truths.

As painting is solely a representative art, either directly reproducing facts, or the laws and forces of nature presented in objects wholly akin to facts, truth becomes most important among its characteristics. To understand the mechanical, vital, and rational forces at work in nature, their distinct methods, and the variety of their individual products, is the imperative preparation for representative art. Correctness is the first element of excellence. That which is falsely done is badly done, though our ignorance may for a time disguise the failure. The painter who knows not the principles which give value and order to nature's action, and does not most carefully mark these as the very substance and power of all his work, stands in alliance with no fact, no real existence, and can only mislead the judgment and pervert the taste. His power lies in the fulness of the truth reproduced under his brush. Though he may neglect particular facts, he cannot neglect the laws which are in all facts, — in the facts of the painting as strongly and visibly as in those of nature. Nature rules in good art with the same absolute and perfect sway which she exercises over things. This is the truthfulness and the value of representative art, that it works under a keen, accurate apprehension of the nature and method of actual forces. Ignorance is the destruction of painting; and knowledge, copious and careful, its prerequisite. It must have science, experience, observation, that it may have beauty. Thus only can it reach its object, — the powerful presentation under their visible symbols of the healthy action of natural, of physical and spiritual forces.

As there is great variety in the facts which the world presents, and as some of these indicate the pleasurable and right action of the forces concerned, and others the reverse, the painter must understand that which is just in expression, and elaborate the successes and not the failures, the virtues and not the vices, of nature; otherwise his art, no longer a fine art, shares the decay and debauch of evil, and works downward as readily as upward. Art in the service of indiscriminate passion, like the honey in the carcass of the lion, becomes unclean, and through the taint of decay loses its native sweetness. We need especially to insist on that which is healthy and right in the theme, so often has painting overlooked it. Art must work with nature, not with her adversaries. All the forces of resistance and perversion which spring up in the pathway of vigorous, of virtuous nature work against her beauty, in working against her wisdom and right. Though passion, like perverted appetite, may take pleasure in wrong, the healthy taste more and more rejects it, and the art which seeks to commend its product to a high and correct æsthetical judgment will be cautious of moral taint, open as it is to the double condemnation of weakness and wickedness.

The battle-field, the gladiatorial show, the fox-hunt, and kindred subjects, in their physical aspects and brutal accompaniments, are revolting, and no art that treats them for what they are in themselves merely can ever make them beautiful. It can make them less vivid and real, and therefore less repulsive, but it can never from their cruel details draw any noble impulse. If that which is offensive, merciless, or terrible is to be treated, it must in some way be overshadowed with moral qualities, be lost in the true heroism of the actors, or, at the least, have the dire and prophetic words of retribution written on it. The notion that things displeasing in themselves are suddenly made beautiful by painting is false. We may take a certain satisfaction in a clever resemblance, but the painting has no other expression, no higher power than a kindred scene in nature. There must be the same mastery of reason over matter, of spirit over flesh, in the one as in the other, before there is beauty.

The dignity of beauty needs also to be especially enforced in painting. Every fit thing in nature is not equally worth the labor of the artist. We are not to have a blind mania for painting which immediately attaches a new and strange value to the most insignificant object when reproduced on canvas. The end of the art is not simply to paint, but to paint that which is worth our protracted attention, and so to paint it as that its most valuable and significant thoughts shall be revealed. The labor of the painter, if less than that of the sculptor, is yet very considerable, and is not to be lost on a meaningless object, or an object made meaningless by its treatment. The theme and method are to be judged by the nature and amount of the thought they reveal, and the artist must approve his stewardship in this intellectual aim. Is it worth while? is a question, when broadly put, as applicable to art as to any other investment of labor. Nothing is more worthless than poor paintings, and we shall be relieved of many of these, if we sternly demand thought rather than form, character rather than color. He only can paint who deeply apprehends and feels visible truth, and to train pupils up to this art by classes and seminaries is as impossible as to train them in a kindred manner into acceptable poets. Drawing, and sometimes painting, may indeed be used as a discipline of the eye, hand, and taste; and so used they may prepare the way for, but are not in themselves fine art.

While some scenes, as more significant and valuable, are more worthy of art than others, there is an equally marked difference in their method of treatment. One artist, invited by that which is casual and accidental, compounds his work of trifles and details, rendering the fact before you only too faithfully in its insignificant incidents; another in each transient compound sees character and principle, and bringing these to the surface, imparts breadth and law to what were otherwise limited and trivial. Under the treatment of the one, the domestic scene is an ordinary kitchen, with ordinary utensils and very ordinary people, living in their poor way; under that of the other, it is this and much more. It is a phase of human life, in which the play of human feeling, hope, fear, affection, are seen, — a chapter from the world's experience thumbed by all our neighbors. The one paints the man when his feelings have sunk back into his heart; the other, when his life has arisen to his lips and face. The one paints with commonplace eyes; the other, with the intuitions of the poet. These he uses for our benefit, and paints the world as he sees it. His high powers are put to service, and we are invested with his inspiration. What presents the most to him he chooses, and so represents it that it bears to us the feeling with which he has freighted it. Even the familiar we see as we had not before seen it, for his higher intuitions have laid it open.

Such work, if the mind be normal, has all value, ever lies within the sphere of the painter, for it vigorously presents visible truth, — truth which has already shown its power in stirring and directing the currents of one heart. There must be present in the artist a quick perception of the forces and thoughts at work in the world, of the fears and hopes which make life eventful. Dulness will render all things dull, a dry detail of facts; while a nature filled with emotion will diffuse emotion through all it treats.

The greater truths of the world are for the painter, as for every artist, locked up in man, and this, not so much in man idealized beyond the facts of the world, as exalted and enriched within those facts. Historic virtue, character achieved, heroism reached, are the significant and valuable truths to man, laboring whether in hope or in despair. The portrait has this license, that it may give the features, not in the deadness of a quiescent spirit, but as the seat and instrument of the best in the man's life. So would memory enshrine them, so far may love transfigure them. The historic portrait has this license, that it may utter all that history has before uttered, tracing, under given restrictions, the man as embalmed in the world's heart.

So completely, however, is the full thought contained in all the works of the world, in themselves, in their inferior and higher adaptations,open to the painter, that man ought to be but one among many themes. In the landscape and lower forms of life, if there is less to move the passions, there is also less to disquiet the mind, and repose more profound and exclusively pleasurable is experienced in view of the stretch and magnificence of God's works, than before anything which human labor or character presents. If Nature does not travel as high, she does not descend as low as man, and preserves, in more pure and unsullied reflection, the image first committed to her. God walks amid the trees of the garden. Nature is more ripe in her beauty than man; she now wears her coronal, and is from this point to pass away. Manhood is incipient, a dawn amid the darkness of storms, a bud under the close, hard cerements of winter. Nature, also, in her beauty is God's grace to man, and runs in advance of his character; the bursting out of undeserved love, and, as having in it the divine heart and feeling, it ought to be dear to man. In the range of the visible universe, painting pursues its object, — the worthy presentation of worthy feeling.

The symbols of painting are as copious as its subjects. Form, color, light, and shade are its constant mediums of expression, while motion, arrested in attitude and interpreted by the relation of the figure to surrounding objects, now lends a vigorous effect. Though the entire language of the eye is furnished this art, color is preeminent among its symbols. This is the peculiar and striking characteristic of the painting. Its animation, its vividness, its power over the eye, and its superior impression of life, are due to color.

In the right management of this lie its mechanical difficulties. Pigments, various, well-defined, permanent, and sensitive, are the first demand of the artist. Different centuries and countries have been quite unequal in their mastery of the best material. Painting will greatly increase in worth and dignity as it succeeds in these mechanical conditions, and its work becomes permanent. Painting wrought upon a wall becomes an adjunct of architecture, stoops to the fortunes of the edifice, and loses something of the value which would belong to it as an independent product. Through color is it that the other symbols of expression are reached. Color is modified by form, and these modifications in turn become to the eye the indices of form. The painting avails itself of this fact, and, unable to render form except in outline, gives to the eye its indices. Those complex judgments which we all unconsciously make in expanding the testimony of the eye into knowledge must now be more carefully studied, that the movement may be reversed, and the painter resolve knowledge, facts, into the symbols of vision, meagre in what they are, yet full in what they give.

Every variety of form, in every variety of relation, secures a new and distinct effect on color, and this effect the painter gives. Without passing from his own symbol, he renders in color, through our unconscious judgments, the complete power of form.

So, too, light and shade are reached solely through these modifications. The intensity and position of the light make an obvious record on the color of every object, bringing it out in brilliant surfaces or hiding it in dark shadows; now inviting the eye to this side, and now to that. Light, thus the adorner not less than the revealer of the external world, yet makes beauty intensely subservient to instruction. Objects are more perfectly distinguished, each from each, by a change of color, light working different results on every different surface. Their agreement is also told — of rock with rock, of tree with tree — by unchanged color. Again, the superficial form of each is shown by a further modification of light productive of further variety; their relation, each to each, is revealed by shadows and illuminated surfaces; and this most complex, significant, and wondrous tale is shifted every moment to record the waning hour. Thus, the unending and changing beauty of the world is the inevitable product of that most sensitive element, light, in the hearty and full discharge of its office as a revealer. Beauty is ingrained in the fabric of the world. The many-colored coat which the light weaves from its spectrum for the adorning of nature is also the inevitable result of a medium of knowledge which could not be perfect without this, its changeable and compound character.

This infinite modification of light — this record of facts and relations on light — is the record of the painting, the record of that superior sense, the eye. The basis of all is color. Through this the body testifies its presence, and on its various-colored surfaces, in still further shades, the remainder of truth is written. It is the art of the painter to write his thoughts, as God writes, on the light, and to make that evanishing record, drowned in the night, lost in the flow of time, as permanent as man.

Aside from facts of light, already sufficiently presented, there are certain others to be mentioned.

(*a.*) The intensity of color is much greater in nature than it can be in art. The full sunlight acting upon color gives it a power which cannot belong to unilluminated pigment. In some scenes, therefore, relative truth alone can be reached. The scene is graded to the maximum effect which can be secured, and thus its character, though not its force, is preserved. In her high power, in her full flood of light, floating the clouds after the spent storm, nature works far above art. The fact outstrips the poor ideal, and the ideal, the poorer actual in paint.

(*b.*) The effects of a landscape are very different as we look upon it with the light or against the light, as the shadows are cast from us or toward us. It seems much more bald and naked in the first instance than in the second. The colors are more distinct, soft, and various when mingled with the shadows than when in even, unrelieved light. The difference is akin to that experienced under a vertical sun as contrasted with evening light. All bodies are so uniformly affected by the noontide rays as to make barren and monotonous the most varied scenery. The action of light, as opening into and opening up a landscape, needs to be carefully marked. The one it does when flowing on with the vision; the other, when working its way among objects from a different or even opposite point. The best effect is reached, not so much by strength, as by inequality and contrast of light. This, enhancing color, at once gives greater variety to the eye, and enables it to judge relations more accurately.

(*c.*) Light is of much greater importance in landscapes than in single objects. Single objects, as man, are revealed with few modifications of light; the landscape is interlaced everywhere with its beams, and a most difficult and chief consideration becomes the effect of these on the objects presented. Still more complex and perplexing is the problem in the case of water. All various scenery is chiefly what it is through its power over the light; and as objects become numerous and of less value in themselves, this additional labor is thrown upon the artist, that they are to be treated under a single condition of light. The unity and the vigor of the piece must largely depend upon his mastery of this element, giving unity and beauty in nature. In any landscape, light, with its invisible attendant, heat, is the chief worker, the stimulating taskmaster of all chemical and vital forces. The vapor, the clouds,

the winds, the plants, all quicken their steps at its bidding, and it robes these servants of its will in royal livery. Light is the prime force of the natural world, and for the painter not to know this is to know nothing.

In man, art, passing over to the side of the spiritual and engaged with yet more recondite forces, is in a measure relieved from these general and physical truths. Even in a large painting, where man is treated, we can hardly wish or claim a full, broad, powerful play of natural forces. One or other of these elements when united should be strikingly pre-eminent; either the force of man or the force of nature, not both.

Sufficient has been said of the end and means of painting to establish the assertion, that broad and careful knowledge as well as just intuitions are requisite for the painter. Nature must have been long studied in her symbols, many sketches have been made, the spirit and precise form of her methods have been caught, before the artist can work with her, or do aught that she would not blush to own.

This is not less true in the treatment of man than of that which is lower. There is more that is homely in man than in any other creature. This should be so, for evil has wrought here more than elsewhere. But there are also here traces of all beauty, and these must be studied, if we would not have our idealism degenerate into vapid notions of perfection, if we would not lose that variety which makes man by himself a kingdom. Thought, virtue, appear in the human countenance under limitation, in conflict, and this is the basis of our interest and sympathy. We must study character, — where human character alone exists, if we

would give that manhood to our men for which only they have value. Every face has in it that which is worth the knowing, for it is the record of a spirit under new conditions, favorable or unfavorable. We are not to have an effeminate love for physical beauty, but are rather to content ourselves with stern, hard facts, since this is the stubborn necessity now laid upon us. Not to humble angels, but to exalt men, is our office, and the office of art, and she must learn how to infuse the higher into the lower, how to glorify the lower by the higher, and this can be taught only in the world.

The intellect and heart demanded of the painter must ever assign him a high rank; and these, when wrought into his productions, impart to them commanding moral power. Since this art is without physical uses, it must be exclusively, and all the more severely, judged on its intellectual merits. That which claims to be gold must meet the tests of gold.

The profound questions of mind and matter, of the condition and destiny of man, which wait on all for solution, wait also on the painter. The insight he shall have into these problems of our being, the answers which he shall render, whether hopeful, fearful, or despairing, will give character to his work, and lead him to find in nature and man the forces of evil, the gloomy portents of defeat; or remedial agencies, the promises and imagery of victory. Great art will know of the intellectual and moral struggle in man, will know his enemies, — ignorance and sin, suffering and death, — and will neither fear nor fail to think and speak of these in its work. It will not draw back from the naked, hard, sad facts of life, and, if it be the highest art, will strike into them some light, as of a dawning day. All things will be understood, — the rough, coarse, and wicked, not less than the gentle, the refined, and the virtuous. Nothing will be vapid, nothing unworthy, for under every transient form the deeper, broader relation of objects will be seen.

The painter finds no other limit to the moral and intellectual character of his work than his own grasp of topics.

The innumerable paintings gathered in the many galleries of Europe impress one strongly with the necessity of a high standard in this art. The majority of these works have little interest beyond an historical one. They are oppressive in number: discriminating criticism is tedious; indiscriminate admiration humiliating. There is comparatively little in these great collections that is now worthy of earnest study and sincere commendation. Value of theme and power of treatment, if insisted on as tests, at once condemn the larger part of the innumerable products of this art. Modern painting has passed through all stages of growth in the six centuries just past; and its first productions are interesting merely as they show the point of departure. Under the influence of Byzantine art, its first productions had neither vigor of form nor force of character, but were a conventional and languid presentation of men and women.

Under a series of masters, — Cimabue, Giotto, Leonardo da Vinci, — the human form and face gradually gained freedom, force, character, till, in the time of Raphael, an entire mastery had been secured in the department of bold, vigorous physical expression. Grecian and Roman sculpture, which leave little to be desired in their control of the human form, had greatly aided this result. There remained, however, great deficiencies in the elements of moral and intellectual expression. Between the Madonnas of Raphael, even, there is great diversity: most of them by no means approach the excellence of the Sistine Madonna, the most celebrated of paintings. They retain something of the feeble, passionless expression, the doll-like face, that belong to so many of the earlier Madonnas. Natural objects, in the mean time, received very little attention. Perspective was but little understood; and hence the distance and relation of objects are lost. Christian art was cultivated in common by most of the cities of Northern Italy, each having its periods of excellence and its great artists.

Later, painting passed into Germany, the Netherlands, and France. The art of these countries is mainly subsequent to the period of Raphael, who belongs to the earlier portion of the sixteenth century. The art of Italy was chiefly religious; that of the Netherlands was largely domestic, presenting the familiar scenes and objects of daily life. Humorous and jovial sentiment entered freely into it; and it gained more variety, and, in some directions at least, more expression, than that of Italy. The criticism often lies against it, however, of choosing unworthy themes. The fruits of the garden, the market, or the hunt, often fill the canvas. Landscape-painting received considerable attention both from Dutch and French artists; yet the great works in this department, though most of them are of comparatively modern origin, have suffered much from the loss of color. Indeed, the landscape, in the multiplicity of its details, seems to be affected more unfavorably by any loss of freshness and intensity of finish than are the higher productions which have man for their subject. Some of Turner's paintings, the great

English painter of landscape, are scarcely intelligible. Landseer well illustrates in his treatment of animal life the assertion, that a lower theme, powerfully handled, yields more than a higher theme handled with less vigor. His animals have more character than many another artist is able to give to men. The directions in which modern art has yet much to do lie in the subtle presentation of the great physical agents and effects of the landscape, and of the moral forces of the human soul. Often as Christ has appeared in art, no Christ has yet been painted. The moral conditions of the problem have ever been too great for the artist.

LECTURE XVI.

POETRY. — ITS NATURE. — RHYTHM. — RANGE OF POETRY. — CLASSIFICATION. — HISTORICAL DEVELOPMENT. — METHOD OF TREATMENT. — CHOICE OF SUBJECT. — TRUTH. — SUGGESTION.

THE most radical distinction between prose and poetry lies in the aim of each. The best approved division of our powers is into intellectual, emotional, and voluntary. These several parts of our nature can each become the primary object of address. Though not acting independently, any one of the three may be the chief seat of action, and the effect there produced the aim of composition. We may wish to act upon the intellect by adding to its knowledge, or, directing its process of thought; to reach the emotions, arousing them to stronger, nobler, more pleasurable activity; or to affect the will, binding it to our purpose. These ends, distinct in themselves, give rise to equally distinct forms of composition. Though the first and third are included under one term, prose, the oration is not less diverse and peculiar than the poem, while the dissertation, essay, demonstration, narrative, and kindred forms addressed to the intellect, constitute a third class.

The interior and essential characteristic of poetry is that it addresses itself to the emotions, and rests in these. It translates all things into feeling, colors all things with feeling.

Poetry is passion, — the throb of a sensitive and aroused nature, emotion wrought into speech. Emotion here acts singly, lending itself to no ulterior end; burning for its own heat, brilliant by its own light.

Poetry, having chief reference to feeling, has naturally allied itself to rhythm, and sought to sustain and perfect the flow of the thought by an accurate and measured correspondence with the flow of syllables. Language thus ceases to be mere arbitrary symbols, conventional sounds, aggregated into irregular sentences, and assumes a distinct and peculiar form, in itself a recognizable harmony. Language thus indicates a direct sympathy with thought, and gives an under strain of music to the play of feeling. It is in entire harmony with what has been said of music that it should thus in its rudiments add itself to emotional composition, and everywhere introduce its essential element of measure into poetry.

As measure establishes a decided, an independent movement in the language, as its accents and pauses recur at stated points, it becomes a leading and inclusive law of form, in good poetry, that the accents and pauses of the thought correspond with those of the verse. Each kind of verse having a distinct form, its own flow of sound, the poet must needs unite the thought to this form, so harmonizing them that the accents and emphasis of the one shall correspond with those of the other. Thus, while the expression preserves its own integrity, and has the grace of a completed rhythm, the thought thoroughly adopts it, is as much born into it as the living spirit into its physical organization.

By this play of metre, poetry as opposed to prose assumes a definite, a rhythmical, a musical form. Form, as a recognizable, distinct element, does not enter into prose, while it is ever present in poetry. This appreciable form is secured in English by the stated recurrence of accent, pauses, and rhymes. In some kinds of verse all of these are employed; in others, as blank verse, the first only. As this arrangement renews itself at fixed intervals, the limit within which the measure returns to its starting-point is called a verse. This may consist either of one or several lines. Accents, pauses, and rhymes, being capable of a great variety of arrangements, give corresponding varieties of verse.

Mere accent, furnishing the most simple and independent rhythm to each line, least of all hampers the expression, and, as in blank verse, suffers the sentence to expand itself through succeeding lines, or contract itself at pleasure. Here the measure, appreciable, though not always powerful, in its effect, gives the utmost freedom to the thought, and keeps pace with it in minor melody through all its wanderings. When definite pauses are added to accent, as in hexameter, these, while increasing the rhythm, proportionately constrain the expression. This must now be so ordered that the pause shall rest upon the emphatic words, and shall not separate closely united parts; the whole grammatical structure is thus affected, and the sentences broken up into members of a given length. If rhyme is also introduced, the rhyming words, by marking a return, a completion of the form, also seek a corresponding completion of the thought, and thus lay upon it the burden of a full cadence. This it also does by the emphasis which naturally falls on the rhyming syllable. The presence of rhyme still further imposes upon the verse its own peculiar burden of returning syllables. On account of these restraints, blank verse has become the chosen vehicle of higher and bolder and more independent sentiment, while the other kinds of verse are fitted for thought which wishes to ally itself more closely to expression, to secure a more definite and choice form.

This distinction of verse, though strictly extrinsic, and not pertaining to the essence of poetry, is yet so obvious and convenient that it determines language, and nothing is called poetry which has not assumed one or other of its forms, and all that possesses the form carries with it the name. We thus have poetical prose and prosy poetry.

Poetry is earlier in point of time than prose, and for this reason among others, that, having a distinct form, it may be transmitted in the loose vehicle of speech without change, while prose cannot escape perpetual modification, having nothing to mark its precise expression. Nor is the burden which poetry imposes less readily borne in the earlier than in the later stages of language. The vocabulary of feeling is first and most rapidly enriched. Length of syllables, inflection, and accents are all more heeded while speech is the controlling element, than when a written literature, being the source of law, language shapes itself more to the eye than to the ear.

Poetry has the entire range of feeling, and is as diversified, therefore, as the states of the human heart. The mean, base, and wicked passions are, indeed, no more presentable in poetry than in life, and yet, as in life, they weave themselves into the complex fabric, if only to suffer the scorn and rebuke of virtue. Poetry owes its entire form to one portion of our nature, and is its perfect counterpart, with this exception, that it represents emotion more under its pure and noble than under its impure and debased forms, — more in its aspirations and impulses than in its lassitude and weakness. True poetry cannot sink wholly to the level of life, for, so doing, it wastes its moral and æsthetical power, and ceases to be a fine art. Poetry is passion, yet not so much vulgar passion as passion vivified and transfigured by the remnant of spiritual apprehension and higher good which ever belongs to the poet.

Poetry must receive its principle of classification from our emotional constitution, and its order of historical development from the development of this portion of our nature.

All emotion has reference to an object, the mind is affected in view of something, toward something. Emotions may be divided into two classes: sensational and rational, according to the nature of the objects giving rise to them, or, more explicitly, according to the avenue through which these enter the mind. The senses, the organs of external apprehension, and the reason, the organ of rational apprehension, are each the inlets of peculiar qualities, the sources of diverse emotions.

This distinction gives rise to two classes of poetry, — the sensational and the rational; the one physical in its objects, the other spiritual; the one giving the play of emotion in a world of things, the other, in a world of regulative ideas, intuitive laws. The word sensational as here used has in it no disparagement, but simply marks the external, materialistic character of the objects to which the feeling attaches itself, — marks a poetry which is alive to that which is, rather than to that which ought to be; which travels through a visible, rather than aspires to an invisible, world. These distinct tendencies will show themselves strongly in poetic production, and mark a fundamental difference, both in the impulse which gives rise to the poem and the impulse which it can impart. The highest field of poesy lies in the emotions when under the action of broad, weighty, and pregnant principles ; in the superior, the moral nature, fully aroused by those truths which press its feelings beyond the present and visible into the unmeasured and invisible.

Sensational poetry naturally divides itself into two classes, — that which holds closely to the external object, and that which is more careful to mark its interior, its mental effect, — that which in description and narrative gives objects and events, and that which traces the flow of life, the action of the heart under these. The one is more physical, rendering things as they are, the other more intellectual, giving them as modified in the feelings and impulses of individual life. Aware of the harshness of the words in this application, we shall yet, in the absence of better terms, call these subdivisions sensual and emotional poetry. The division into sensational and rational marks the avenues through which the exciting cause, the subject of poetical passion enters the mind. This in the one class is the senses, in the other and higher class it is the reason. The words sensual and emotional have reference to the subject-matter of the poem, — the one including the external, the substantial and visible, the other the internal, living experience amid things and facts.

These distinctions — like the fundamental distinction between poetry and prose — will not be found to perfectly correspond with those more slight divisions which rest on form, as the song and the sonnet; nor with those which rest on single aims arbitrarily selected from allied aims to the neglect of further classification, as epic and dramatic poetry. While these secondary divisions will surrender a portion of their matter to one, and a portion to another, of the classes now instituted, we shall yet find that this reference of poetry to its distinctive aim, its subject-matter, is more or less recognized in them. Epic poetry, as heroic narrative, presents life under its external, visible forms, in its achievements and successes, and so far is sensual. Dramatic poetry, representing life in tragedy on the side of justice, of retribution and reward, and in comedy, on the side of accident, of the fitful and mirthful, also cleaves to the external, incarnating the spiritual, so far as it attains it, in a sensible, material form. Narrative, descriptive, and pastoral poetry evidently belong to the visible, sensual world.

Lyric poetry, on the other hand, the ode, the sonnet, is more reflective, marks the passion, the internal state, embodies a sympathy, a desire, a hope, and is thus emotional. So, too, the autobiographic poem and satire, didactic and philosophic poetry, so far as these have a right to exist, mark the action of the feelings on external objects, and belong to emotional poetry.

The last class, which more directly contemplates the higher intuitions of truth and right, and more immediately feels their impulse, also includes much that is lyrical, — songs of freedom, of labor, of worship. The impassioned claims of the heart for the higher forms of good, its rebukes of wrong, its sense of offended justice and hastening retribution, its calm trust in ultimate issues, its aspirations, its adorations, are all emotions, arising strictly under its spiritual nature, and looking, not to the visible, but the invisible for satisfaction. The reason of man, moving amid great principles, will, from time to time, lift the heart of man above that which is agreeable, pleasing, hopeful, up to that which is purely and transcendently rational, truthful, rightful.

The historic development of poetry is for the most part in the order of the classification now given. The external and material, in its most material form, first occupy the passions, and we have the romance and the ballads of the middle ages, or the stricter epic of the early Grecian culture. Life in its retributive and disciplinary character is later seen, and thus later furnishes the matter of the drama, — in form belonging to the sensational; in spirit, often a prophecy of the purely rational. The ripening reflective powers, no longer yielding all to the active impulses, give lyrics, those voices of the interior life, uttering what one mind has thought and heart felt amid the din of action. The inner life must strongly have asserted itself as against the outer life, have been able to affirm the prior worth of its own experience, and have gathered up, in the rest and silence of reflection, the evanescent phenomena of the spirit, before the lyre will be strung for their utterance. Culture must have made very considerable progress before poetry will pass from the visible to the invisible, from the material to the intellectual. Yet more must there be of training, before our fundamental intuitions, deep principles of order, shall so govern our thinking as to call forth the profoundest, holiest feelings, as to make the broad, the moral relations of action the theme of our most impassioned verse. In times of great conflict only, when men are searching for their rights, when religious natures are wrapped in a holy enthusiasm for fullest, highest truth, or in the inspiration of devotion, will the strength of spiritual impulses show itself in poetry.

Each of the several classes now enumerated admits of very diverse methods of treatment. The sensual may stand out grossly on the sensual side, description may be mere description, narration mere narration, giving all things in their visible and material aspects; or, with more quick apprehension and susceptible feeling, the poet may especially single out those features which affect the heart, and everywhere reach the more significant and expressive points of things and actions. The drama may sink, loathsome and lost, in the mere filth of life, the detail of vice, or with unflagging justice, scourge the criminal, and cleanse away the moral ichor. So, too, emotional poetry may vacillate between philosophy and passion, between dry, acute analysis and the pulsations of a changeable, susceptible, vigorous life. It may forget its just function, and become didactic, or, with a truer apprehension of its mission, it may unveil without destroying the phenomena of a rich interior life. Rational poetry also has its range, sinking or growing in merit. It may be perceptive, coolly cognizant of law, the sharp censor of guilt, or render the emotions of a profoundly moral and religious nature in view of great rights and great wrongs, — of purity and impurity, of immutable truth and blind, mutable passion.

Each department is equally open to great poetry, and the great poetry of each department is most akin in its impulses, in its hold of the invisible and vital.

Our remaining thoughts we can best present as distinct considerations in the office and character of poetry.

(*a.*) Poetry especially shows its inclination upward or downward, its power or want of power, in its choice of subjects. It cannot accept and apply itself to the tasks of history and philosophy without ceasing to be poetry. Indeed, such a choice of themes indicates that the poetical spirit does not exist, that a vain effort is being made to preserve a form whose life has escaped.

The past is generally supposed to have certain advantages over the present as the field of passion and imagination. Facts obscured by time, less apparent in their precise outline and features, yield more freely than passing events to the conception, readily receiving shape under the poetic imagination.

These and kindred considerations are often urged against the present, practical, and commonplace, as rendering it of necessity unpoetical. These conclusions are, we apprehend, pushed too far, and that the present offers some peculiar advantages to poetry, and has some peculiar claims upon it. Different ages are not so much poetical or unpoetical in their external conditions, in their transient circumstances, as in their intellectual character, their emotional life. When poetical power is present, it will in every age find abundant objects on which to exercise itself, while, without it, every phase of life will be wearisome monotony.

Chivalry in itself was oftener a brutal, passionate, and loathsome commonplace than either the magnanimity of benevolent virtues or the exaltation of manly courage. It is what it is to us largely through the transforming, transfiguring power of the poet. A cruel fact has become a brilliant fiction. Poetry complains that she is not able, that she is not at liberty with her high fancies, so to transmute and glorify the present. On the other hand, we would rather say that this is her precise office, her highest mission, and that the subduing feeling, the earnest experience which should ever be the leading characteristic of poetry will readily do this very thing.

The poet, that he may be eminent, must first be pre-eminent in native forces. His feelings cannot go groping in blind passion, but must have the sharp vision of a quick intellect, and rational intuitions. His thoughts cannot remain inflexible crystals, but, dissolved in feeling, must be ready to recrystallize around every new nucleus given to them. Without profound passion and deep experience, the poet has no poetry, and can render none that does not in barren description cling to the surface. With this inner under-current of an aroused and sensitive life, the present, far from being a dull monotony, will be the gathered strength, the treasured value of the past, the pregnant transitional moment in which all forces, concurrent and conflicting, are writhing and wrestling to shape a yet unrendered future.

The present, as it is the home of life, of effort, of power, is the true home of passion. Thither the battle-field and the tocsin of war are transferred, all else is deserted, — is death. On these plains the dusty armies of men, wasted and torn by the conflict of centuries, at length debouch. Here, where work is to be done, victories gained and lost, where alone are the wails of woe and the shouts of joy, the poet should not, the true poet will not, complain of the want of impulse and feeling.

Only by this apprehension of the present, this pulsation of his life with the life of the race, by which the throes of every new birth go rending through him, can the poet become a worker, a prophet, a bard, whose martial songs stir deeper and ring louder than drum or fife. How can a poet have inspiration who is ever with the dead, and this, only that he may cherish their forgotten pomp? Or, if he have inspiration, why should he expend it in this valley of bones? The past restored will often be but a flimsy fiction or haggard ghost.

If human life as a reality, a passing and eventful reality, has no interest, no value, certainly restored in dreamy fiction it will have less interest, less value. He who has not fathomed the current of life which bears him onward, who has not felt its forces or been whirled in its eddies, is certainly unable to treat poetically the themes and objects of the hour; but this is no proof that these have not in them superior passion and interest.

Pre-eminently are these considerations just in connection with all poetry that springs from impulse, and lends impulse, that feels the action of law and principle. These are the forces at work in the present, and with gathered clearness and strength struggling into mastery. Poetry that arises from moral and religious emotion will have to do with the present.

The poem has historical value which reflects the life of its times. This value is lost if each period, weary of itself, is to seek that which is most alien to its own spirit, if, no longer rendering itself, its experience of joy and sadness, it is ever retreating to realms of fancy. Nothing is more indicative of hopeless and intrinsic poverty than ennui, a perpetual weariness of the thing that we are, that is, — and this, not as wrong, but as vapid, not as misdirected, but as without direction and import. That period does best that best renders itself, that is full of its own action, inspired by its own success.

Even the epic, with its strict adherence to the external, is less and less able so to handle the past as to renew it in the affections of the present. A great epic will hardly again be written on the basis of warlike exploit, of brute strength, or military passion. If nothing heroic can be found in a commercial and intellectual age, then the heroic scarcely remains to us, since the physical heroism of former times is passing more and more from our affections. The epic of a literary and Christian people must proceed on the notions of that people, trace its conflicts, and mark its endurance, and honor its successes. If we are destitute of that nobility of spirit which strives with enthusiasm and waits with patience, we have fallen below the epic; but if not, if there is yet that in action which can justify and sustain the passion of poetry, he deserves most of his age who works this virgin gold of high endeavor into a coronet, the crown of past success, the lure of further effort. Light up the life that is with the virtue that is, or ought to be, and bear not forever the inspiration and imagery of poetry, as pure oil pressed from the best life of the present, back to the censor of an old, worn-out hero-worship. This claim of the present upon poetry is more and more recognized, and will be recognized by all whose ears catch the tread of events, who know that life flows no more shallow, no more muddy, no less sublimely, than in times of yore, when eddying on through strife of battle.

(*b*.) Not less important than the theme in poetry is its

method of treatment. There are few subjects which have not in them a vein of poetry, since there are few themes which do not at some point touch the heart. On the other hand, there is no subject so exclusively, so transcendently passionate, as not to be capable of becoming a dry skeleton under anatomical treatment. It is the peculiar function of the poetical mind to apprehend all things on their living, emotional side, and so apprehended there is poetry in them all. The quick intuition and aroused heart do not fail, because they put their possessor in connection with the sensitive and the vital; deeply conscious of every pulsation in the world's life, he is able to transmit it. With an extended and delicate surface of auditory and visual reception, no movement escapes him, the deep under-current or the surface ripple. Armed as with a stethoscope, his ear is pressed close to the throbbing breast of man; armed as with optic glass, his sharp eye wanders far and near, searching the play of mighty and minute forces. It is this superior perceptive power, this delicate musical tension of every emotional chord, that makes the poet more than another, that makes him our interpreter, the revealer of our blind impulses, our truer, nobler consciousness. These better gifts, this inspiration, the poet is bound to have and to exercise in our behalf, otherwise he is a conjuror without his wand, a king without his sceptre, a prophet with no divining spirit. Better far to look on the external world through our own eyes, than with the dull, cold, languid eye of another. The poet only blesses us when he teaches us how a mind, ranging on broader wing, piercing with sharper vision, more justly open than our own to pleasures and sorrows, hopes and fears, views the world within us, the world about us, when he brings light to paths in which we had before groped, when he sets ajar the gates which had too much sundered us from the unseen. Why should he be our guide, who bears no torch? Why should the poet sing that knows no melody?

He who lacks this very substance of poetry, emotional thought, will most frequently strive to supply its place with the mere mechanism of verse, with labored expression, sharp antithesis, and novel phrase, all indicative of an effort most thoroughly self-conscious of feeble thoughts, fully occupied with the etiquette of language, like prim personages of fashion, lost, ingulfed in the very act and courtesy of living.

(*c.*) Truth presses the same unyielding claim on poetry as on painting or sculpture, and this in some new particulars. The painter must make all things consistent with the one passion and the one moment he has chosen to utter, but the poet must also understand all the fluctuations of feeling, and be able to trace its phases, — to mark correctly its growth and decay, its abrupt and consecutive transitions, and to keep the expression ever afloat on the current of the heart; nor this alone under one set of circumstances, but under all circumstances, — not alone in one character, but in all characters. In epic and dramatic poetry, the insight into human life must be accurate and broad, to meet the conditions of truth, to keep imagination, in its most powerful movements, within the limits of law.

The claims of truth are not inconsistent with that rule of reason which poetry maintains amid its passion; those superior impulses which it imparts to its heroes. While closely wedded to the world that is, it is also cognizant of the world that might, and shall be, and delights to give its creations a movement thitherward. Thus does it become a moral power, impatiently striving with the actual, not that it may escape it, but that it may correct it.

Akin to this, also, is the increased, and so far the unnatural, dignity and scope of language which the drama allows her characters. It is not, as we have all along seen, in the barren fact, in the mere vulgar actual, that poetry delights, but in this illuminated by its own interior light, transfigured in obedience to a higher law of its own nature, apprehended under its better impulses. The poet transfers to the language of the clown and the villain his own apprehension of them respectively. He washes them of their filth, and leaves them before the eye in the bold, clear lineaments of character, since this alone we are in search of. He shows us what is significant or powerful in them, and, beyond this, wipes them away, as simply offensive and burdensome. The physician, passing the detail of disease, merely directs the eye to that which is symptomatic.

The cleansing power of pure science, pure truth, is remarkable; certainly that of poetry, of pure beauty, should not be less so. The sunbeam that lingers in the cesspool is not tarnished thereby. Not even the beetle has the taint of carrion. No man works more from within than the poet, and, according to the want of intrinsic purity in his own life, will be the soil which he will contract.

While speaking of the claims of truth, we need to remember that truth in poetry is exceedingly distinct from truth in philosophy in the form which it assumes. The one seeks the naked principle, the other the facts which contain and express the principle. The one draws attention to the law, the other to the phenomena under the law. It thus often happens that a spirit of poetical criticism is not only not identical with, but opposed to, the true spirit of poetry; that the mind thereby falls away from the exuberance of life, of feeling, into the sharp analysis and restricted statements of the intellect; that the element of thought in its effort to be correct grows upon the element of emotion, robbing it of its spontaneous impulses.

Truth in poetry is unconsciously held, a living force, working in a living way for its own ends, and of its own power. Truth in philosophy is the aim and determined product of the mind, the result of destructive distillation. The poet does not simply understand character, thereby formally working out given results; he possesses it in its impulses, and these realize themselves in a distinct, natural, truthful growth. He presents new experience, bold character, and just phenomena under familiar principles and old forces.

(*d.*) With increasing culture and the transfer of thought and interest from the near and sensual to the remote and supersensual, poetry more and more deals with suggestion, demands a quicker apprehension and an aroused imagination. as conscious of addressing minds more critical in their action and broader in their knowledge. Poetry is thus less simply narrative, less plainly descriptive, closely cognizant of recondite passion, deeply reflective of interior life, subtle in its grasp of illustrative imagery. This tendency in poetry calls the mind into more vigorous action, and rests the effect largely with the receptive power of the reader. The task of Milton was by no means so simple as that of

Homer, but success was no less possible and grand with the first than with the second. The growth of refinement and knowledge, indeed, sweeps away some material of poetry, but adds other material as apt and forceful as any that has been lost. That which is, is not less impregnate with beauty than that which the half-cultured mind thinks to be. This growth makes the labor of the poet more difficult, but also gives him superior strength wherewith to perform it. We have faith in poetry; we have faith in man's nature. The one does not live merely amid the phantoms of twilight; the other does not grow into barrenness, does not ripen into a hard, rugged, half-worthless fact. Poetry is permanent; springing from the soil of the heart, it there ripens into well-rounded and beautiful life. It is the fulness of art, ranging through the representative and creative imagination. Dealing with arbitrary symbols, it suffers no limitations but those of feeling and language.

THE END.

www.ingramcontent.com/pod-product-compliance
Lightning Source LLC
LaVergne TN
LVHW010230110826
845151LV00004B/1248
9781425524838